Alternative Therapies & Reiki Miracles

By
Swami Ramesh Chandra Shukla
Reiki Grand Master

Published by:

F-2/16, Ansari Road, Daryaganj, New Delhi-110002
☎ 011-23240026, 011-23240027 • *Fax:* 011-23240028
Email: info@vspublishers.com • *Website:* www.vspublishers.com

Branch : Hyderabad
5-1-707/1, Brij Bhawan (Beside Central Bank of India Lane)
Bank Street, Koti, Hyderabad - 500 095
☎ 040-24737290
E-mail: vspublishershyd@gmail.com

Follow us on:

For any assistance sms **VSPUB** to **56161**

All books available at **www.vspublishers.com**

© **Copyright: V&S Publishers**
ISBN 978-93-505706-1-6
Edition 2013

The Copyright of this book, as well as all matter contained herein (including illustrations) rests with the Publishers. No person shall copy the name of the book, its title design, matter and illustrations in any form and in any language, totally or partially or in any distorted form. Anybody doing so shall face legal action and will be responsible for damages.

Printed at : Param Offseters, Okhla, New Delhi-110020

"The part can never be well unless the whole is well." ~ *Plato*

Publisher's Note

After a number of bestsellers on Health, V&S Publishers have now come up with this unique book named Alternative Therapies & Reiki Miracles. The book has been authored by Swami Ramesh Chandra Shukla, an exponent and veteran in this field. In this book, the author has tried to combine the Reiki miracles with other alternative therapies. Reiki Master, Shri Rajesh Gupta has also given his valuable inputs in giving a concrete shape to this book.

Basically, **Reiki** is a *spiritual practice developed in 1922 by Japanese Buddhist Mikao Usui*, which has since been adapted by various teachers of varying traditions. It uses a technique commonly called *palm healing or hands on healing as a form of alternative medicine* and is sometimes classified as *oriental medicine* by some professional medical bodies. Through the use of this technique, practitioners believe that they are transferring the *universal energy* (i.e., Reiki) in the form of *Qi* (Japanese: Ki) through the *palms*, which they believe allows for *self-healing and a state of equilibrium*. There are **two main branches of Reiki**, commonly referred to as **Traditional Japanese Reiki** and **Western Reiki**. All these have been elaborately discussed by the author in the book.

So, **Reiki does not just provide a permanent, natural and spiritual prevention or cure to a disease, but aims at complete eradication of the disease from the root-level in certain cases.** It awakens your life force energy and heals your body, mind and the soul.

Therefore Dear Readers, Read on to explore the world of Reiki and Learn these powerful postures or exercises as prescribed in this altogether magical Alternative Therapy to boost your energy at all levels, be it physical, mental, emotional or spiritual.

Foreword

Health is seen as a state of harmony or balance in the organism. Negative influences in one's life are thought to throw the body out of balance and create illness. Various complementary and alternative techniques have been developed in recent times. Among them, *Reiki* has a major role to play. It is an *independent healing therapy* and it can be also combined with other healing modalities.

    I have attempted to combine Reiki miracles with other alternative therapies. The present book is the result of my this effort. In making this book useful and popular, we have given details of many alternative therapies in short and *Reiki therapy* in detail. In preparing this book, Shri Rajesh Gupta (Reiki Master) has helped me a lot in giving this book a concrete shape. I owe my thanks and blessings to him. I think that this book will prove a milestone in the field of Reiki and other therapeutic healing. The book is of own kind and therefore, I expect that it will be welcomed by all interested in the therapy field.

– **Swami R C Shukla**
Lucknow

Contents

Publisher's Note 5
Foreword 7
Introduction 11

Lesson 1
About Reiki – What Reiki is and isn't, History, Bipolar Nature of Reiki 17

Lesson 2
Uses of Reiki in Everyday Situations 24

Lesson 3
Five Principles of Reiki 28

Lesson 4
How to Heal with Reiki — Preparations, Treatment Methods & Reiki 30

Lesson 5
The Human Energy Body — Meridians, Aura & Chakras 38

Lesson 6
Hand Positions to Heal Self & Others 50

Lesson 7
Short Treatment, Group Treatment & Chakra Balancing 57

Lesson 8
Emotions & their Locations in the Body. 65

Lesson 9
Treating Common Ailments with Reiki 69

Lesson 10
Other Energy Exercises 72

Lesson 11
Advanced Reiki 75

Lesson 12
Techniques & Tips 108

Introduction

In modern times, when medical science has reached to such ahigher dimensions, the role of complementary and alternative therapies cannot be denied. According to a scientific survey nearly 1/3rd of the population believes and uses such therapies for their health problems.

A large number of such therapies are being used. Along with old types, new types of such therapies are being invented and practised nowadays. I give here a list of such therapies with details of some of them.

My purpose is to make these therapies more popular, effective and useful if they are applied with Reiki.

Reiki is such a wonderful tool that it can be added to any alternative therapy to make it more useful and effective.

So besides giving the list of such therapies, I shall give details of some such therapies. The main alternative therapies prevailing nowadays are many but I am giving only 47 of them.

List of other therapies

1. Aroma Therapy
2. Alexander Therapy
3. Autogenic Therapy
4. Acupuncture
5. Acupressure
6. Auriculo therapy
7. Bach Flower Remedy
8. Colour Therapy
9. Chiro Practic
10. Craneal Osteopathy
11. Chinese Herbal Medicines
12. Christian Therapy
13. Crystal Healing
14. Cell Level Healing
15. Diet Therapy
16. Dance Therapy
17. EFT
18. Flower Essence Therapy
19. Herbal Medicine
20. Hypnotherapy
21. Hugging Therapy
22. Iridology
23. Laughter Therapy
24. Meditation Therapy
25. Music Therapy
26. Massage Therapy
27. Magnet Therapy

28. Meta Healing
29. Naturopathy
30. NLP
31. Osteopathy
32. Polarity Therapy
33. Psycho Therapy
34. Past Life Regression Therapy
35. Pranic Healing
36. Quantum Touch Healing
37. Rolfing
38. Reflexology
39. Shiatsu
40. Sexual Therapy
41. Spiritual Healing
42. Tai-Chi-Chuan
43. Tibetan Healing
44. Theta Healing
45. Visualisation Therapy
46. Vastu Pyramid
47. Yoga Therapy

Now let us take up some of the above therapies which are very relevant with reference to their application with Reiki Healing.

1. **Aroma Therapy**

   Aroma therapy is the use of *essential oils* and *hydrosols* to promote healing and personal health. When used with Reiki, it works wonders.

   Aroma therapy combines the sciences of Chemistry, Botany and Physiology with the use of essential oils to achieve physical, emotional and mental balance and healing as well.

   The term, *Aroma Therapy* was *coined by the French Chemist, Rene Maurice in Aromatherapic* published in 1937.

2. **Alexander Technique**

   It is a powerful technique and process of awakening self awareness of movements in its relationship to health and well-being. The process is more educational than therapeutic. This technique helps to balance the spine, mobility of joints and increased flexibility of body movements.

3. **Acupuncture**

   The word *acupuncture* originated from the Latin word, *acu*, which means *needle* and *puncture,* a term proposed by the Dutch Physician, *William Ten Rhyne*. It is the method to treat diseases by inserting fine needles into precise points called *acupuncture points* located along the energy channels.

4. **Acupressure**

   The Chinese discovered that pressing certain points on the body relieves pain. *So the Chinese Physicians developed this technique of curing certain illnesses by pressing or piercing* certain points of the body. Acupressure when combined with Reiki works wonders.

5. **Bach Flower Remedies**

   Dr. Edward Bach discovered these wonderful healing remedies.

   There are 38 Bach Flower Remedies. They are Agrimony, Beech, Centaury, Cerato, Cherry Plum, Chestnut Bud, Clematis, Crab Apple, Elm, Gentian, Goose, Heather, Holly, Honeysuckle, Hornbeam, Impaliens, Larch, Mimulus, Mustard, Oak, Olive, Pine, Red Chestnut, Rock Rose, Rock water, Scleranthus, Star of Bethlehem, Sweet Chestnut, Vervain Vine, Watnut, Water Violet, White Chestnut, Wild Oat, Wild Rose and Willows.

   These are *38 essentials that heal from deep within*.

6. **Colour Therapy**

   Healing with colours is a very effective therapy produced from very ancient times in India and foreign countries. In the *Chakra system* of healing colours, also refer to specific *Chakras* as under:

The Chakras	The Colours
Base	Red
Sacral	Orange
Solar Plexus	Yellow
Heart	Green
Throat	Blue
Brow	Indigo
Crown	Violet

   The Colour Therapy uses variety of measures for diagnosis and treatment. In Reiki, the practice of *Chakra* balancing, colours, etc., play a useful role in healing.

7. **Chiropractic**

   The ancient healing practices were usually performed by priests. The spine was seen as a lifeline for various energies that flowed throughout the body. Dr Palmer developed the philosophy of *Chiropractic*. He developed it into the unique healing method.

8. **Crystal Healing**

   Crystals are also very useful in healing. Many Reiki Masters use these crystals for healing. They have developed a different and very useful system in healing by the use of crystals.

Crystal therapy is now a separate branch of learning.

9. Diet Therapy

It is based on the idea that diet and foods have also healing powers. If used properly, they can heal us. This therapy is now used on a large scale even by doctors.

10. Dance Therapy

Dance movement therapy is an excellent healing art. It uses movements of the body to heal it. It affects us on all levels, physical, emotional, mental and spiritual.

11. EFT

Emotional Freedom Techniques (EFT) founded by Gary Craig is an Energy Psychology Technique based on Ancient Eastern Energy and Modern Psychological Tools. According to Gary Craig – The root cause of all diseases is the disruption in body's energy system. This uses tapping by finger tips on certain acupressure points while repeating a basic statement several times.

12. Herbal Medicine

Herbal Medicine is the use of whole plants or parts thereof for the treatment of diseases.

13. Hypnotherapy

Hypnotherapy is very popular nowadays for healing unresolved issues related to health and life.

14. Laughter Therapy

Many tensions of life are washed away by the use of this therapy.

15. Music Therapy

Music therapy is very useful in treating emotional problems. This therapy is limited to three areas: Neurology and music, The nature of the music experience and The role of the music therapist. Musical activity activates several senses simultaneously.

16. Meditation

Meditation is also used for therapeutic purpose if combined with Reiki and it gives miraculous results.

17. Massage Therapy

This therapy is one of the oldest existing discipline. Nowadays, *Kerala Massage* and *Thai Massage* are practised very much.

18. Magnet Therapy

Magnets are also used for healing several diseases.

19. Naturopathy

In modern times, Naturopathy is very popular which is practised on a larger scale.

20. Past Life Regression Therapy

This therapy is used to resolve our past life traumas. It works on our cellular memory level.

21. Pranic Healing

This science has developed in modern times with Reiki Healing. Pranic Healers often combine Reiki healing with them.

22. Polarity Therapy

Polarity therapy is a comprehensive health system which includes and incorporates body work, diet, exercise and counselling.

23. Psychotherapy

In modern times, psychotherapy is considered as a medical treatment for the brain/mind. *Medical psychotherapy* was originally based in *Freud's psycho-analytic theory.*

24. Reflexology

Reflexology is the therapy that deals with the principle that there are reflex areas in the feet and hands which correspond to all of the glands, organs and parts of the body. This method uses thumb and fingers to apply specific pressures to these reflex points to achieve therapeutic benefits.

25. Rolfing

Rolfing is a holistic philosophy, science and art of releasing pain and chronic stress.

26. Shiatsu

Shiatsu is a Japanese word meaning finger (shi) and pressure (atsu). A Shiatsu treatment stimulates circulation and flow of lymphatic fluid, releases toxins and removes deep-seated tensions.

27. Spiritual Healing

Reiki is very helpful in dealing with spiritual ailments. *It is a science of the soul.*

28. Vastu Pyramid

Pyramids are used for correcting defects of Vastu in houses

and offices or factories.

29. Visualisation Therapy

Visualisation therapy is a powerful tool that invokes an inner mental picture usually using all the senses which include vision, hearing, smell, touch and taste.

30. Yoga Therapy

Yoga is a very powerful tool nowadays to heal our physical, mental and emotional illnesses. Many other therapies are also used such as *Panch Karma, Pranayama, Asanas* to accelerate good health. Reiki is also very useful for such ailments when combined with Yoga.

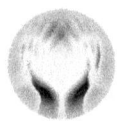

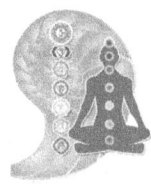

LESSON 1

About Reiki

What is Reiki?

Reiki (pronounced Ray-key) is a Japanese word. *Rei (Ray)* means universal and *ki (key)* means life force energy or spirit. Ki is also named *Chi by Chinese, Prana by the Hindus, Holy ghost by the Christians, Bioplasmic energy by Russians, ka* by the Egyptians, Pneuma by the Greeks, Mana by the Kahunas, Yesod by Jewish Cabalistic Tradition, Baraka by the Sufis, Fluid of life by Alchemists and the Healing power of Nature by Hippocrates.

Reiki is a great complement to all kinds of medical treatment. *This includes conventional medicines, chiropractic, homoeopathic and herbal.* Reiki does not introduce any substance into the body and works largely by supporting the body's ability to heal itself. *Reiki is a modern way to relieve stress, improve your health, inner growth and stay youthful.* Reiki works inside the conscious and subconscious mind of every human being giving back the state of original wellness to both mind and body.

Reiki is the life's force or energy. Awakening your Chi across your mind, body and spirit to all be cancelled instead of operating in fragmented parts so that they work harmoniously.

- Einstein and quantum physicists have explained that at an atomic level, everything that exists in the universe is energy.
- Physical matter and energy are just two forms of the same thing.
- Human beings are also made up of electromagnetic energy.
- Every cell, atom and subatomic particle that makes up the human body is vibrating at different rates depending on their biochemical make-up.
- Electromagnetic output can be measured in humans.
- Normal biological frequency for the human body is around 250 cps.

> Between 400-900 cps in people used healing energies, such as Reiki.

Scientific Proof

This research has 'proven' what has been accepted spiritual wisdom of many cultures for thousands of years *that an unseen energy flows through and connects all living things.*

Belief in existence of universal healing energy that promotes healing in humans, plants and animals.

Practising Reiki allows you to leave chronic illness behind. It allows you to go from an external centred life to an internal centred life.

So in learning Reiki, you will heal your physical discomfort, emotional imbalance, mental stress resulting from blockages in energy flow. It also heals blockages formed by negativity, own thoughts towards, how others behave towards us, fatigue, self talk and poor physical care. You will also:
> Awaken your life force energy.
> Heal your body, mind and soul with *chi*.
> Learn to balance your thoughts and emotions.
> Learn powerful exercises to boost energy at all levels physical, mental, emotional and spiritual.

What Reiki is not

Knowing what Reiki is not is as important as knowing what it is.

1. *Reiki is a spiritual energy not a religion. Religion and spirituality are two different things.* Reiki can be practised and received by people of any religion.
2. *Reiki is not massage or reflexology.* Reiki is an energy healing system and not a manipulative system (hands moving the body). Reiki is distinct from reflexology and massage. Reiki is simply omnipresent but we are not aware of it until we contact it through an initiation or attunement.
3. Reiki may incorrectly be seen as a tool for the practitioner rather than the practitioner being a tool for the Reiki to move through. A practitioner who believes that energy is a tool, something to use for healing or spiritual growth is one who believes he is in control of energy. This can lead to a practitioner diagnosing or judging what is best for the client, which in itself can lead to an attempt on the practitioner's behalf to offer an undue influence on the client. This is not considered to be beneficial or ethical for either party.

What Does Reiki Do?

From time to time, your energy may get thrown out of balance, whether it be from illness, stress, poor diet, or emotional issues. Reiki can help balance your life energy, and therefore, help heal any self-induced or stress-related disorder. Reiki works best in conjunction with your regular health practitioner, and can be administered by yourself or another practitioner as often as needed. Unlike modern or herbal medicine, you cannot overdose, become allergic, or reject Reiki, 'as energy is nature.' Energy is what we all are at the core level, like water is a necessity of all life forms. Reiki can help heal injuries, speed the process of recovery, and even assist in resolving emotional issues. *There are no limitations to Reiki.* The path of Reiki allows us to express impersonal love through universal love. First it teaches us to love ourselves.

Reiki can help alleviate suffering, whether it is of a physical, emotional, mental, or spiritual nature. This means that Reiki can heal. This statement is not a guarantee or a promise that someone will be relieved of any illness (it is illegal and immoral to diagnose unless you are a medical doctor). However, in most cases, Reiki does stimulate improvement whether used in conjunction with either traditional or holistic medicine, or even all by itself.

Sometimes people have unreasonable expectations of Reiki, both as clients and as practitioners. Reiki cannot promise to produce an instant miraculous cure for any condition. That does not mean I have not seen my share of spontaneous healing, but results like this are in the hands of the client and his or her ability to ask for healing, and not only the power of Reiki. *Like other modalities, it can take time to see long-term results.* Reiki works with you to restore energetic balance and repair things like blockages and tears in the energy field that create disease and unhappiness.

How is Reiki different from other healing methods

Reiki is a form of energy medicine. The essential difference is Reiki's utter simplicity. One has to learn how to listen to one's hands. It is a recognition that no one ever heals anyone else. All healing is pure grace and just happens. It is a recognition of our true state of non-doing. Reiki attunements or empowerments are essential ingredients in Reiki. At the first degree level, there are four attunements and at the second degree and third degree, one attunement respectively.

History of Reiki

Up until recently, Reiki was passed exclusively via oral tradition. Due to this, there are many variations in the story of Reiki, as well as missing pieces to the emergence of Reiki as we know it today. We do not know the exact details involving Mr. Usui's quest for Reiki nor the exact circumstances that lead him on his initial quest.

Mikao Usui was born on August 15, 1865 in Taniai, Japan. He was always a spiritual seeker. He practised Kiko, which is similar to *Qi Gong* or *Chi Kung, Kiko,* consists of breathing exercises, meditation and movements. It could be described as a 'moving meditation'.

He studied medicine, psychology, religion, and spiritual development. He was a member of a metaphysical group called Rei Jyutu Ka. Mikao Usui became secretary to Shinpei Goto (the head of the Health and Welfare Department who went on to become the Mayor of Tokyo). Usui sensei started a business, which failed. In 1914, at the age of 49, he decided to become a Buddhist Monk. In 1922, he went on a 21-day retreat of meditation, prayers, chanting and fasting at Mount Kurama in Kyoto, Japan. While standing under a waterfall, he did a meditation designed to open and purify the crown chakra. This caused him to have a spiritual awakening on the final day of his retreat. A powerful light entered the top of his head. His awareness was expanded and he realized a great power had entered him. Before him appeared five symbols in the colours of the rainbow.

Mikao Usui says about Reiki "Work on your heart and do things from the quite space inside you. Anyone can access Reiki because it begins within yourself.

The meanings and uses of the symbols were communicated to him intuitively, spiritually, from a Higher Source. Hawayo Takata brought the Usui System of Reiki from Japan via Hawai to USA and Canada. Starting at 1970 Takata trained twenty two new Reiki Masters before she died.

The Spiritual Nature of Reiki

Reiki, as a system of energy exchange, is very much connected with living a spiritual life. While this does not require any specific religious practices, nor should it ever conflict with your personal belief system, Reiki often enhances one's attitude of life and Spirit.

The observer within - Reiki helps your growth process by

developing an independent observer within. You learn detachment whereas being attached to people, things and results are constant source of all your miseries.

To me Reiki is a very deep spiritual sadhana. It is not technique oriented but love oriented. Jesus says God is Love, I go a bit further and declare that Love is God. Love is ENERGY. God is also an energy, he not a person but a presence. Energy can never be separated from its Source. You cannot experience God directly but you can certainly experience love and energy so instantly. Reiki is a journey from visible to invisible and it is really very spiritual.

Energy is an expression of frequencies, vibrations or waves at different speeds. Energy moves in waves, i.e., in cycles per second. We use *Hertz* as a measure of cycle per second. Every cell in the body emits a frequency. *Reiki is an Energy Science.*

Reiki teaches you to detach from your negative body obsession.

Reiki teaches love, respect and gratitude for the body. The body is your basic truth. Of course you are more than the body, but that more will follow later on. First you are the body but you have been taught to be and work against the body, forgetting that this is a gift from God. Reiki's first lesson is to love your body. Love your life. Always affirm your inherent goodness value and beauty. Reiki teaches about being a unique you.

Reiki makes you whole. To be whole is to be holy. At present you are living in one dimension of life(i.e. the physical). Other dimensions are missing. Reiki teaches you to live in all the three dimensions of life - physical, mental and spiritual.

As Reiki is not only physical, it frees you from all types of obsessive body attachments. Reiki teaches to go beyond the body, as it opens the door of your other dimensions of being. Always remember:

1. Reiki is not learnt in the usual sense, but is transfered from a Reiki Master to his students during a Reiki Class.
2. Reiki use is not dependent on one's intellectual capacity or spiritual development and therefore is available to everyone.

Living spiritually means 1. Awareness 2. Detachment 3. Unconditional Love 4. Responsibility 5. Surrender and letting go 6. Gratitude, etc. Through Reiki our spiritual journey actually starts in the truest sense.

You have three centres : 1. Being the Centre 2. Feeling the Centre and 3. Thinking the Centre. Reiki covers all the three centres but it gives more importance to the heart than the mind. Every beat of the heart is putting 2.5 watts of power. *It is creating an electromagnetic field. This is not an aura.* The field that radiates out from your heart has been measured by current instruments up to 3 feet away or beyond. In contrast, electromagnetic energy of the brain only goes about an inch outside your head. *The heart's magnetic energy is 5000 times more powerful than the brain's.*

Always remember that you live in a vibrational universe — Everything is a vibration from thought to thing and miracle of Reiki is that it enhances your levels of vibrations immensely.

Some Reiki masters recommend some power tools of Reiki to maximise the power of Reiki. They are: Gratitude, Giving, Present Moment Awareness, Intention, Detachment, Basic Relaxation, White Light Meditation, The Heart Process, Centering, Affirmations, The Reiki Prayer, Salt Water Bath, Aura Cleansing, Motherly Touch, Angelic Healing, Shamanism, Reiki Essences, Reiki and your higher self, Acupuncture, Aroma Therapy, Massage, Bach Flower Remedy, Ayurveda, Yoga, Chi Kung, Crystal Therapy, Colour Therapy and Dowsing etc.

Why have a Reiki treatment?

Reiki heals at all levels: Physical, emotional, mental, spiritual.

On a Physical Level

1. Soothing: Gentle and relaxing
2. Raises energetic vibrational level
3. Supports body's innate ability to heal
4. Boosts immune system
5. Improves functioning of the endocrine system. Toxins are released.
6. Highly successful in dealing with aches and pains.
7. Headaches, backaches, arthritis pains, personal injuries, effects of drugs reduced, etc.

On Emotional Level

1. Creates deep sense of well-being
2. Increased optimism
3. Positive attitude towards life
4. Promotes greater ability to deal with everyday challenges

On Mental Level
1. Counteracts incessant chatter of mind
2. Deeper thought processes accessible
3. Awareness
4. Facilitates decision-making abilities
5. Promotes mental clarity in general
6. Easier to avoid distractions, improves focus on tasks.

On Spiritual Level
1. Clients may experience their own spiritual side
2. Sense their own uniqueness
3. May sense that connection to everything else
4. Feeling of expansiveness
5. Practitioner may receive messages, images and may contact to their higher selves.

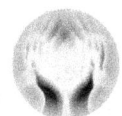

Uses of Reiki in Everyday Situations

1. Helping plants reach their potential
2. Boosting your food, water and medicine
3. In automobile and computer problems
4. Abundance (money, etc.) through Reiki. The difference between rich and poor is not in how much money they have but in the way they talk, the way they act and the way they think. The way you think is what you create your inner and outer world.
5. Gratitude helps in generating abundance in all areas of your life. Gratitude opens your heart and connects you and aligns your vibrations to that which you feel grateful for and as such ,attracts more of the same into your life.
6. Cleaning and clearing out negativity of clutter, rooms and space
7. Protecting your loved ones
8. Healing your home with Reiki
9. Healing Vastu defects
10. Memory, study and interviews
11. Healing relations
12. Helpful in negative self talk for personal growth. We program our mind by managing and changing our negative self—talk with Reiki
13. Missing articles and persons
14. Alignment of the Conscious and the Subconscious mind— The subconscious mind processes about 400 billion bits of information per second and the impulses travel at a speed of up to 100,000 mph. Compared to this your conscious mind, which possesses only about 2000 bits of information per second and its impulses travel only at 100-150 mph.

Your conscious mind is almost dim-witted cousin of the subconscious mind. So long as your conscious mind is not aligned with your subconscious mind , nothing will happen. If your conscious mind wants something and your subconscious mind wants something else, it is impossible to create what you want.

15. Reiki helps balancing the left and right hemispheres of the brain as well.
16. Combining Reiki with prayer, meditation, intention, visualisation and affirmation. Prayer is more than meditation, In meditation, the source of strength is one's self. When one prays, he goes to a source stronger and greater than himself. Super-focus is the focus so complete that you are not even aware of that you are focussing. So much absorbed like reading a book that is a super-focus state. Maintain a super focus state for long enough until your subconscious mind is programmed to attract your goals towards life. Scientific research shows that the average person cannot focus on a single thought for longer than 6 seconds at a time. Thus, it is a big problem if you are trying to use *conventional visualisation.* Remember, you cannot program your conscious mind. Your subconscious mind can be programmed with thought patterns and belief systems. Research shows that 76% of an average person's thought are negative. Reiki is very helpful. If you experience stress, you will not be able to program your mind with your goals. Remember your subconscious mind cannot be programmed effectively until you are totally relaxed. If you cannot relax, you cannot attract.
17. Balancing your *chakras* with Reiki.
18. Reiki helps the dying person to adjust internally and to prepare to die with dignity and peace.
19. Use Reiki in hospitals.
20. Use Reiki in accidents, emergencies, surgery, chemotherapy and radiation. Reiki helps to reduce the side effects of drug therapy.
21. Treating babies and children. Many children are very receptive to Reiki energy.
22. Treating the elderly. Reiki is very effective for elderly persons in their physical mental and emotional well-being.
23. Treating pets and animals.
24. *Reiki can combat ageing.* Reiki cannot change your chronological

age but it can alter your functional age. You are as old as you feel. *Age is a state of mind. If you feel old, then you are old.*
25. Reiki is very helpful and useful during pregnancy and labour. Reiki heals the baby before birth.
26. Developing your intuitions.
27. Finding your soulmate with Reiki.
28. Overcoming addictions and using Reiki to change habits.
29. Reiki and other therapies—Reiki enhances the effects of acupressure, acupuncture, aromatherapy, massage, bach flower remedies, Ayurveda, Yoga, Chi Kung, Crystal Therapy and Colour therapy as well.
30. Reiki balances your yin and yang energies and so it minimises your gender-distinction, the cause of evil and cravings.
31. Reiki may heal the karmic bonds - If the client has an illness due to his/her past *karmas*, Reiki can do the healing without interference with the *karmic* process.
32. Cutting etheric cords through Reiki : The *chakras* often have etheric cords protruding from them. These cords which look like surgical tubing extend to chakras in other people with whom we had relationships. Etheric cords act like horses, with energy directed back and forth between both people. Therein lies the problem with having them. If the person wit whom you are attached is having a life challenge, that person will siphon energy from you. He or she will draw upon your energy through the etheric cord. You will then feel drained without knowing why.

Inner management through Reiki: Reiki makes you whole. *To be whole is to be holy.* We are holistic beings with natural talents and capacities and in all our four dimensions—physical, mental, emotional spiritual. Reiki supports all dimensions of your being.

Reiki for Enlightenment: Reiki also offers us the opportunity for spiritual development. *It is much more than a therapy – it is multi-faceted practice that when used on a daily basis, feeds the soul.* It includes prayer, meditation, concentration and love. To me Reiki is a deep spiritual *sadhana* that begins from the visible body but reaches up to the invisible soul. Reiki helps us meeting our true self. Through practice of Reiki, our ego's mask vanishes and we connect to our inner self. Reiki opens the communication with the Higher Self (Super Conscious mind).

Reiki is a new way of looking, thinking and feeling about yourself and your self growth journey. You don't have to destroy every cloud to see the sky. All you have to do is to keep remembering that you are the sky.

Now Look at the Main Benefits of Reiki:
- Releases stress and anxiety
- Amplifies energy
- Balances energy
- Reduces pain and suffering
- Helps release emotions
- Heightens creativity
- Increases awareness
- Minimises feelings of fatigue
- Improves sense of well-being
- Boosts the immune system
- Increases and strengthens physical vitality
- Enhances feelings of peace and relaxation
- Releases old patterns of behaviour that keeps you stuck
- Can be learnt easily

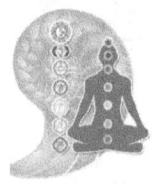

Five Principles of Reiki

The principles of Reiki are a guide to harmonious living, and abiding by them can be healing in and of themselves. Mr. Usui noticed that those who benefitted most from Reiki, practitioner and clients alike, were those who actively embraced a spiritual set of principles in their daily lives.

These guidelines, often referred to as the Reiki Principles are:

Just for today, I am free of <u>anger</u>

Just for today, I am free of <u>worries</u>

Just for today, I am working <u>honestly</u>

Just for today, I am <u>loving</u> to all living beings

Just for today, I am <u>thankful</u> for my many blessings.

Incorporate these Reiki Principles into your daily life. The most important part of Reiki Principles states, "Just for today". Practise these principles today. Tomorrow will be another today and you can start over again. The Reiki principles are to be chanted in the morning and evening. It is not enough to just read the Reiki principles. You must aim to live by the *Reiki Principles.*

The importance of these five spiritual principles:

These principles are the heart of Reiki. There are a number of variations. Popular versions of these principles are:

For today only -

Do not anger

Do not worry

Be humble

Be honest in your work

Be compassionate to yourself and others

The Reiki Principles as Key to Awareness

The five Reiki principles were originally outlined by the Japanese Meiji emperor as spiritual guidelines for the Japanese people. Later, they were adopted by Dr. Usui to help and serve as guide posts to greater awareness for his Reiki students.

I want to make some things clear. They are as follows:
- You are not healing.
- The system is not healing.
- What is healing then?
- First your intention
- Secondly your love towards the people who need healing.
- Third, your alignment with the spiritual power connection with the spirit behind.
- Finally, the destination or the path of the one who receives the healing.

LESSON 4

How to Heal with Reiki

Healing is of two types

1. Touch - 7 methods
1. Palm touch
2. Finger touch
3. Massaging
4. Stroking
5. Tapping (fist & Finger)
6. Pressing actual points of pain
7. Directing energy flow

2. Non-touch – 16 methods
1. Aura (2-3 inch from body)
2. Beaming
3. Distant healing
4. Sweeping (Whole Area and Local Area)
5. Cleansing (Anti-clockwise)
6. Charging (Clockwise)
7. Blowing
8. Seeing with the Third Eye (Gazing)
9. Anchoring and Drawing
10. Rotational Healing (Imagining rotation of *chakras*)
11. Lotus Healing (Imagine finger as lotus petals)
12. Laser Beam (A mere imagination that laser beams are channelised from finger tips to dispel diseases)
13. Psychic Surgery
14. Trident Healing

15. Merging with aura (Merging your aura with another person's aura and infusing energy)
16. Vedic Healing

Steps in Healing

1. Prayer (Invoking Blessings)
2. Protection
3. Imagine yourself in a white light pyramid with master above you protecting you
4. Actual healing with affirmation and visualisation

Frequency of Healing of Organs

Nerves heal at frequency of 2 Hz

Bones heal at frequency of 7 Hz

Ligaments heal at frequency 10 Hz

Capillaries heal at frequency 15 Hz

Healer's hand 0.002 GAUZ (1000 times stronger than other body parts.

Stress Hormones

1. Cortisol
2. Dopamine
3. Adrenaline

These are released in to the blood stream during stress. Reiki helps in this matter to a great extent.

What is Treatment?

Treatment is the process of cleansing one's body and mind through touch. This healing process, as it is called, is divided into three segments, all the three take place simultaneously.

(1) Scanning

(2) Charging

(3) Counselling

Hence energy is not confined to infusing energy alone.

Methods to increase sensitivity in the nerves of your hands

1. Imagine receiving cosmic energy by raising both hands towards the sky. Then bring both the hands in front of your *heart chakra* in a prayer position. Repeat the process three times.
2. Create an imagination that you breathe with your hands. This equips the hands to inhale more energy.
3. Think that the earth infuses energy through your legs.
4. Shaking of the hands and legs sidewards and up and down respectively, ensures the smooth flow of energy.
5. Even joining both the hands together can enable you feel the magnetic rays between them.
6. Rubbing both the hands increases the vibrations between them.
7. Rotating hands (left) clockwise or anticlockwise and increasing the sensitivity of the right hand can be done and this movement should be akin to a dance step.

When one does *Reiki healing,* the energy is guided by the higher power and does not require direction from the practitioner. Therefore there is no concern about whether the healing is being done properly as the higher power always guides the healing energy in a way that is exactly appropriate for the client.

Scanning - Scanning a person's body before the treatment can help determine where energy is most needed. To begin stand alongside the person with your hands 5 or 6 cms above the body moving slowly along the length of the body from head to foot. Notice any area that feel especially warm or particularly cool. Be aware of the sensations in your hands and concentrate on your hands' experience as they move over the body. Do they feel tingling or prickling in a particular area? While scanning remember that you are working in the person's energetic field or aura where it is possible to sense imbalance before they manifest physically. By this technique, you can detect where the energy is needed. Notice where your hands encounter a subtle difference in body temperature. You can interpret impressions in the following ways.

Heat: It indicates energy is needed. Spend more time on this area. Thus heat will dissipate during treatment.

Coolness: There can be an emotional or emotional energetic block.

Hands feel repelled from an area. It indicates deep-rooted issues the person is reluctant to face.

Sharp pain: This indicates build up of energy in the area.

Tingling: It indicateds inflammation.

Vibration: It may indicate a *Chakra* imbalance.

Sweeping: Sweep down the energetic field to clear the energetic debris released during treatment. Place hands 6 or 7 cms above the body. Imagine that any energetic toxins are being absorbed into the earth are melting away into the ether.

After your first or singular attunement, it is highly recommended that you practise self-healings every day for 21 days prior to working regularly on others, in honour of *Mr. Usui's 21 days of solitude.* Just because the attunement is done does not mean that you have mastered the system! *Reiki takes a lifetime to truly master.*

Grounding and Centering

1. Sit in a comfortable position.
2. Rub your palms together for few seconds and place your hands on your thighs or in a prayer position.
3. Close your eyes and take few deep breaths.
4. Visualise Universal life force energy or Reiki in a form of pure bright white light entering your *crown chakra* at the top of your head.
5. Let this pure white light move down the body refreshing, energising and revitalising each cell of the body.
6. Visualise this re-energising the vital energy descending down through all major *chakras* down to the *root chakra* taking care of each surrounding cell.
7. After reaching the *root chakra* or *Mooladhara,* this white light now enters into the ground towards the earth's centre.
8. While inhaling, visualise that energy is entering into the body through the *crown chakra* and while exhaling, it leaves the body through the *root chakra* into the Earth.
9. Now Cosmos, You and the Earth are all in one alignment duly grounded and centred.

Setting the Intention to do Reiki

Just like going to work or school, you need to prepare to do Reiki. You need to set the intention and warm up before you can lay hands. There is no right or wrong way to do this. Simply say to yourself that you are ready to do Reiki now, and that is all you will ever really need to do. When you are done using Reiki, say so again and thank the Universe/God for allowing you to be a channel of these energies.

Self-Healing and Living with Reiki

Reiki heals every aspect of our lives. It is a practice that cures our illnesses, soothes our emotions and enables us to create the life that we want. Giving yourself healing is a very important aspect of Reiki. It is strongly recommended that you perform self-healing regularly, preferably daily for the first month as well as improving your health, it will balance and centre your mind/body/spirit system, thereby allowing for a dramatically increased flow of Reiki energy during healing sessions. Most importantly, it will definitely increase your inner guidance, helping you to cope with everyday situations more successfully, as well as providing spiritual guidance when appropriate. It is also advised to trade out regular healings with fellow Reiki practitioners, massage therapists, etc, to keep your mind, body and spirit, pure and vibrant.

The pictures of hand positions are given on a separate page that suggests self-healing routine. You will be placing your hands in a number of different positions on the body. Spend around 3 to 5 minutes in each of the hand positions. It is important to follow these guidelines at first. Once you are familiar with the basic procedures and have gained confidence, let your hands be guided by your intuitions.

Practise, experience and patience will surely bring you to the stage where you can trust your inner guidance. In any case, the universal energy is always overlooking your healing sessions, ensuring that none of your attempts will ever go unrewarded.

It is suggested for those who have difficulty sensing their own Reiki to do the following:

While fully clothed, place your hands on your *heart chakra*, over your clothing.

Take a deep breath and relax.

Sit patiently in this position and set the intent to open your hands to channel Reiki to your heart (chakra). It is likely that you will need to sit patiently in this position much longer to feel the first sensations of Reiki – possibly as long as 30 minutes.

However, if you relax and allow it, it will flow! Then once you know exactly how your self-Reiki feels, you will always sense it, and the response time will be faster each time.

Before healing 1) Rub your palms together. 2) Press your palm *chakras* with the thumb of the other hand. 3) Press your finger tips against the finger tips of the other hand. 4) Cup your hands and place them on your knees with palms facing upwards. Keeping you eyes closed proceed as follows. 5) Create an imagination that you are breathing with your hands. This equips the hands to inhale more energy. 6) Think that the earth infuses energy through your legs. 7) Even joining both hands together can enable you to feel the magnetic rays between them. 8) Shaking hands and legs sideways and up and down respectively ensures the smooth flow of energy. 9) Rotating the hands left clockwise or anticlockwise and increasing the sensitivity of the right hand can be done, and this movement should be akin to a dance step.

Attitude of Gratitude

1. I thank myself (name ....) for being here.
2. I thank the cosmic energy or Reiki for being here.
3. I thank my parents (name ....) for being in my life.
4. I thank my Guru (name ....) for always being in my life
5. I thank my God (name ....) for always being in my life.

   In case, you are treating others, thank him/her for accepting Reiki from you.

   Then start Reiki work by saying 'May Reiki flow for healing.'

Reiki Finish

When the client has accepted all the Reiki needed at one session, conclude his treatment with the *Reiki Finish*.

a) On completion of the treatment of the front of the body, draw anticlockwise energy spirals with the index and the middle fingers on the body of the patient beginning at the shoulders down the arms to the finger tips, and from the shoulders down along the side of the body to the tips of the toes.

b) After the treatment of the back of the body, give Reiki to both the soles and then balance the energy in the spine. Then sweep the energy quickly and forcefully down the spine (for diabetics sweep the energy up the spine, i.e., in the opposite direction).

   Wash your hands again, or press your finger tips together for 30 seconds to close down the energy flow.

Protect yourself from negative influences while sleeping through Reiki

1. Put granite under your bed. Get four pieces and put at the four corners of your bed. Black tourmaline is also good. You may keep it in your pocket also.
2. Envision the shield of white light.
3. Imagine the energy being deflected and then grounded rather than bounced back to the sender, otherwise the energy will come back to you.
4. Call on Archangel Michael for protection.
5. Place salt on each and every window.
6. Place mirrors on each wall with their reflective surfaces outward rather than facing into the room.
7. Drawing out the Reiki protection symbol and placing it under your pillow.

When Not to Use Reiki

1. Reiki neutralises anesthesia quickly. So do not use Reiki beforesurgery or dental work.
2. Do not use on broken bones until a doctor has set them. Otherwise bones may join before right placement.
3. Do not use on a severed limb until it has been re-attached. The energy can seal off the veins and nerves making it hard to re-attach the limb. In these cases, it is all right to treat other parts of the body, such as the adrenals for shock.
4. If you are Diabetic, Reiki can reduce the amount of insulin you need to have, so let your doctor monitor your dosage.

Do not use Reiki immediately after taking any medicine or else it will neutralise the effect.

Rules of Reiki

1. Don't consider yourself as a doctor.
2. Don't give Reiki, make it available.
3. Don't force Reiki on anyone.
4. Don't give Reiki for free. There must be an exchange of energy for the time spent for you.
5. Don't be attached to the results.
6. Reiki requires no diagnosis.

7. Never take up a healing as a challenge.
8. Never doubt Reiki even if the desired results may not appear immediately. Reiki has its own intelligence and works accordingly.
9. In no way should a practitioner take advantage of the therapeutic relationship.
10. Can Reiki be used with other healing methods? Reiki stands on its own as a self-contained healing method. It does not need to be combined with any other technique to improve it.

Healing Time

The time spent on each point for healing is 3-5 minutes for adults (full body session will last for 90 minutes). For infants and children, the total Reiki time is 10-15 minutes.

Children below 8 years of age may not be given attunement as their energy fields are not developed and so immature attunement is harmful.

LESSON 5

The Human Energy Body

Meridians

There are three basic components of the human energy body– *Aura, Chakras* and *Meridians*. There are *35 meridians* in traditional *Chinese medicine*. The *12 major meridians* are each related to a specific organ in the body. They are not connected to the organ itself but instead to the function of the organ. So there are heart, lungs, kidneys, meridians and so on. We must know the lunar cycle of the body as well as the daily rhythm of the solar cycle. Energy is constantly flowing around your body and the flow of ki peaks in each of the 12 major organs for 2 hours each day as follows :

1. Heart — 11 am - 1 pm
2. Gall bladder — 11 pm - 1 am
3. Small intestine — 1 pm - 3 pm
4. Liver — 1 am - 3 am
5. Urinary bladder — 3 pm - 5 pm
6. Lungs — 3 am - 5 am
7. Kidneys — 5 pm - 7 pm
8. Colon — 5 am - 7 am
9. Pericardium — 7 pm - 9 pm
10. Stomach — 7 am - 9 am
11. Triple heater — 9 pm - 11 pm
12. Spleen — 9 am - 11 am

Frequency of Healing of Organs (Hz)

Nerves heal at frequency = 2
Bones heal at frequency = 7
Ligaments heal at frequency = 10
Capillaries heal at frequency = 15

Healer hands frequency = 0.002 Gauz (1000 times stronger than from other body parts.) Dr. Andra Puharich was able to measure an 8 Hz magnetic pulse coming from the hands of the healers. He found that healers who produce a more intense signals have a greater effect of healing. Dr. Robert Beck, a nuclear physicist measuring the brain waves of the healers found that all healers during the process of healing exhibit the same wave patterns of 7.8-8 Hz. He also found that during the healing moments the healer's brain waves become both frequency and phase synchronised with the earth's magnetic field called the Schumann waves. Healers are also able to take energy from the magnetic field of the Earth for healing the patients. The latest invention from UK is a computer based system using a video camera technique wherein the energy flows from the fingers/palms of the healer entering the energy field of the patient's body can be seen live on the monitor.

Human Aura

The Aura is an invisible field that surrounds and interpenetrates the physical body along with the *Chakra system*, *Meridians* and *Nadi's* supplies our physical body with the Universal Life Force Energy. This is made up of much finer and lighter vibrations. It is most commonly called the *aura,* the *auric field*, or the *human energy body.* This energetic aspect of our Self can sometimes be seen by some clairvoyants and healers, who may see different colours in the energy field around a person.

Anatomy of the Aura

1. Shape of the Aura
a. The Round shape (looks oval)
b. The Square shape
c. The Pointed Oval shape at both Top and Bottom

2. Division of the Aura
(a) Health division (b) Mental division (c) Emotional division (d) Magnetic division (e) Colour division (f) Spiritual division

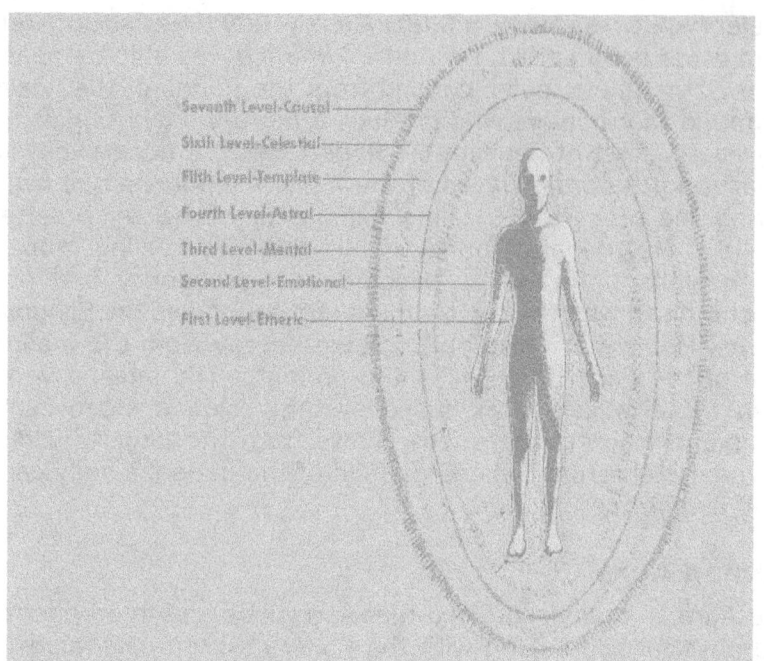

The Aura briefly consists of various layers of energy, which are vibrating at different rates, the closest level to the physical body the Etheric Level being of the densest vibration. These layers are known as :

1. Etheric Body (Red)
2. Emotional Body (Orange)
3. Mental Body (Yellow)
4. Astral Body (Green) This fourth body is the body where spirituality really starts.
5. Etheric Template Body (Blue)
6. Celestial Body (Indigo) &
7. Ketheric (Violet)

The seven *chakras* belong to men's seven subtle energy bodies

Generally, a distinction is made between:

1. The Spiritual Aura which has a diameter of 15-18 feet.
2. The Mental Aura which has a diameter of up to 8 feet.
3. The Etheric Aura which radiates from the physical body to a length of about 8 inches.
4. The Aura can be photographed by the *Kirlian Camera* which was discovered by *Semyon Kirlian of Russia* in 1939.

Since these auras overlap, it is not always possible to determine them individually.

Aura Chakra Connection

Each *Chakra* is intimately connected with the aura that surrounds it and the state of the Chakra has therefore a profound impact on the person's aura. The first layer of energy closest to the body has the densest vibrations, and these grow lighter and faster as the layers get further away from the body.

Two divisions of Aura: (1) Outer Aura works as a shield 6-8 feet or more (2) Inner Aura — (4-6 inches or more) healing, cleaning and Reiki is addressed to this inner aura.

How to see Aura

There are two ways in which we are able to see the aura of another human being or pet or even an inanimate object. *The first is by simply observing it with your eyes and the second is by observing it with your mind's eye.* However, there are three simple ways to practise seeing aura with your relaxed eyes.

Method 1

Sit and gaze at a plant or tree against a plain backdrop, such as a clear sky. Trees have very strong energy field.

Method 2

Hold your own hand up against the sky and spread your fingers wide. Look between the fingers and around the outlines of your hand.

Method 3

Ask a friend to sit or stand against a white wall. Keep the light dim and observe what you can see around the body.

Extension of Aura: (1) Ordinary Humans — 6-8 feet (2) Healthy and intelligent — 8-20 feet (3) Meditative person — 40 feet or more (4) Jesus, Krishna, Buddha, Mahavir, Muhammad — 300 kms

Kirlian Photography

- The aura can be photographed
- Made up of layers
- Each person's energy field is a unique signature of that person
- Auras can show how that person is; mentally, physically and emotionally

> An aura expands and contracts depending on how you are feeling

Aura Cleansing

An aura cleansing takes only a few minutes and can be done with person standing up, sitting down or lying on a bed. The most convenient position is standing up. To do aura cleansing, first activate the healing energy in your hands. Next visualise your hands becoming large brushes with 2-4 inches (5-10 cms) bristles coming out of your palms. See and feel your hands becoming the brushes.

In an aura cleansing, always keep your hands 2-6 inches away from the person's body and never touch the body. Since auric field extends beyond the physical body, start with your hands about 12 inches (30 cms) higher than the top of the head and parallel to the body. Do not hold your hands directly over the top of the head so as not to interfere with the person's connection with their higher Self. Bring your hands straight down the entire length of the body all the way down to the feet, allowing your hands to touch the floor. As you move your hands, visualise the brushes that your hands are removing all the negative energies from the energy field. Always brush the energy from head down towards the feet. Complete each sides, then move clockwise around the person until all the four sides have been cleansed.

The Chakra System

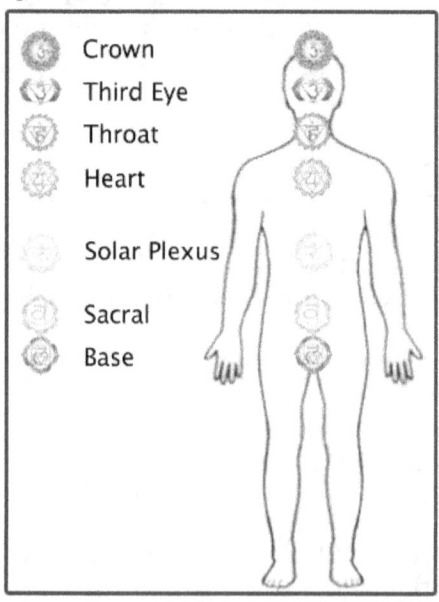

Chakra is an ancient Sanskrit word meaning the **wheel**. *Chakras* are our energy centres. They are the openings for life energy to flow into and out of our aura. Their function is to vitalise the physical body and to bring about the development of our self-consciousness. They are associated with our physical, mental and emotional interactions.

There are *seven major chakras.* The aura is often referred to as the *eighth chakra. The first chakra (root) actually hangs outside of your body.* It is located between your thighs, about halfway between your knees and your physical body. *The seventh chakra (crown) is located on the top of your head.* The remaining chakras, (sacral, solar plexus, heart, throat and third eye), are aligned in sequence along your spine, neck and the skull. Individually, your *chakras* look similar to funnels with petal-like openings. *Chakras* are invisible to the human eye, but they can be perceived intuitively by trained energy workers. The seven principal *chakras* correspond to seven basic personality types. Know the dominance of a particular *chakra* in your body.

Complimentary Chakras

Each chakra has a special relationship with one another *chakra.* It is so called *complementary chakra.* Their energies stand in the strongest opposition but also work to complete each other. The one exception is the *Heart Chakra* which does not have *complimentary chakra.* Standing as it is at the centre of the *chakras,* it has no opposite poles.

Crown and Root, Third Eye and Sacral, Throat and the Navel are *Complimentary Chakras.*

Chakra	1st	2nd	3rd	4th	5th	6th	7th
Name	Muladhara (Root)	Swadhisthan (Sex)	Manipura (Navel)	Anahata (Heart)	Vishuddhi (Throat)	Ajna (Third Eye)	Shasrar (Crown)
Location	at the tailbone	2 inch below navel	belly	center of the chest	bottom of the neck	center of the eyebrows	entire top of the head
Petals	4	6	10	12	16	2	1000
Endocrine	Gonad	Gonad Adrenals	pancreas	Thymus Imunesyst.	Thyroid	Pineal	Pituitary
Elements	Earth	Water	Fire	Air	Ether	Space	Light
Planets	Saturn	Venus	Mars	Sun	Jupiter	Mercury	Moon
Color	Red	Orange	Yellow	Green	Blue	Indigo	White, Gold, Violet
Mantra	Lam	Vam	Ram	Yam	Ham	Om	Aum
Sense	Smell	Taste	Sight	Touch	Hear	Clairvoyance	Cosmic consciousness
Function	Survival protection	Sex relations, emotions	Power, Creativity	Love Compassion	Communication, Self expression	Intuition, Intelligence	Spirituality

Note : Each major *chakra* on the front of the body is paired with its counterpart on the back of the body and together they are considered to be the front and rear aspect of *one chakra*. The front aspect is related to person's feelings and the rear to his will.

Scanning the Chakra : If you want to test your own *chakra* to make sure they are working efficiently, you can scan them with a pendulum, with the palms of your hands or mentally looking at each *chakra*.

Exploring Chakras and Awakening Your Untapped Energy

Chakra Healing and Meditation

Chakras are centres in the human body. These energy centres are neither physical nor anatomical. They are found in the subtle energy system, although their radiant energy does correspond to position within the body. The *chakra*s influence cells, organs, and the entire hormone system and affect one's thoughts and feelings.

Chakras are associated with particular colours, symbols, *mantras*, elements and deities, which correspond to their vibratory frequencies.

Ailments due to Chakra Blockages, Check up and their Activating Processes

1. Root Chakra

Ailments related to blockage : Digestive disorder, Hemorrhoids, Constipation, Lower back pain, Sciatica, Skeletal problems, Osteoporosis, Pain in the legs and feet, Varicose veins, Anaemia and other blood disorders, Stress induced ailments, Allergic reactions.

Check up : When you need to work on your *root chakra*

    If you feel you have lost trust in life

    If you don't feel at home in your own body

    If you worry about the future and meeting your obligations

    If you feel like you are losing your emotional footing

    If you feel chronically tired and lacking in energy

    If you often feel cold or have cold hands and feet

    If you have problems with your colon and your digestion is not working properly.

    If you suffer from sciatica or throw your back out

Activating Root Chakra

Exercise regularly. Get physically active.

Enjoy a foot massage on a daily basis. Knead the soles of your feet forcefully.

Practise *Titili Asana* and *Sishupal Asana* for 10 minutes.

Spend as much time as you can outdoors. Take long walks and go barefoot whenever you can.

In the morning, bathe your upper and lower legs in cold water.

Wear red clothing and use red fabrics in your home. Place red flowers around the house. Learn to play drums and enjoy sunset.

2. Sacral Chakra : By strengthening your *sacral chakra,* you will raise your joy in living, creativity and sensuality.

Ailments related to blockage : Prostate problems, Impotence, Sexual ailments, Kidney problems, Bladder and urinary infections, Lower back pain, Cyst, Inflammation of the ovaries, Uterine problem and menstrual pain, pain in hip joints.

Check up

If you don't enjoy life

If you suffer from sexual problems and don't feel sexually fulfilled

If you lack appreciation for life and don't recognise its beauty and poetry

If you feel, your creativity is blocked

If you suffer from jealousy and feelings of guilt

If you are very hard on yourself and put too much importance on discipline and self-control

Activating Sacral Chakra

Get in contact with water. Take baths, go swimming, or walk by a lake or a rivers, a sea or ocean.

Drink enough liquids like mineral water, juice or herbal tea.

Wear orange clothes, put orange flowers or oranges in your living room.

Go dancing.

Embrace your sensuality and take aromatic baths, use scented body oils or take steam bath.

Listen to Eastern music.

3. Solar Plexus

Ailments related to blockage: Stomach ailments or ulcers, Heartburn, Diseases of the liver, spleen and the gall bladder, jaundice, Stomach ache, Disorders of the digestive tract, backache, Nervous disorders, Obesity, Anorexia

Check up

If you suffer from anxiety

If you are overweight or you suffer from eating disorders

If you have jealous or aggressive tendencies

If you suffer from nightmares or insomnia

If you feel difficulty in expressing your feelings freely

If you have a hard time recognising goals and/or reaching them

If you give in to others too easily

If you have a hard time accepting criticisms

If your emotions get the upper hand and you do things that you later regret

Activating Solar Plexus

Get into contact with the fire elements. Try to relax near a fire place. Light candles in your house.

Romantic music strengthens the solar plexus.

Learn how to express your feelings.

Employ the practices that aim at strengthening the solar plexus.

Stay warm, especially in cold weather.

Make sure you breathe from your stomach, not from your chest. Open yourself to the sun's power: Enjoy short but regular sun bathing and consciously take in the solar energy.

Bring the colour yellow in your life. Buy yellow clothing, sheets and place settings. use lemons as a decorative element in your house.

4. Heart Chakra

Ailments related to blockage: Coronary illness and angina pectoris, High and Low blood pressure, Elevated cholesterol, Arrhythmia, Heart attack, Inflammations or Infections of the lungs

Asthma and other respiratory problems, Allergies, Cold, backache in rib cage area, etc.

Shoulder pain, Skin problem, Rheumatism in the arms and hands.

Check up
If it is difficult for you to let other people into your life
If you feel lonely or isolated
If you have relationship problems
If you have problems sustaining friendships
If social situation leave you tired and worn out
If you have a hard time wholeheartedly accepting yourself

Activating Heart Chakra
Love yourself. Treat yourself in a loving way.
Take loving care of others.
Get in touch with the beauty of nature. Hug trees. Feel the influence of the colour, green.
Wear green clothing: Decorate your home green. Make sure there are plenty of plants in your home.
Listen to the music that touches your heart.
Learn to embrace and comfort other people.
Employ the sense of touch, such as Reiki.
The *new moon* and the *full moon* phases are the ideal times for activating your *heart chakra.*

5. Throat Chakra
When your throat chakra is strong and free of blockages, your heart and head will work together with harmony.
Ailments : Tonsillitis, Dental and Periodontal problems, Trouble with the vertebrae in the neck, Neck and shoulder pain, Overactive or under active thyroid, Speech defects, such as stuttering.

Check up
If you suffer from shyness or feel uncomfortable or inhibited in the presence of others
If you have hard time expressing yourself
If you suffer from any kind of speech defect
If you have a tendency to be manipulative
If you have hard time telling the truth or often find yourself telling white lies

If you don't feel inspired by your work

Activating Throat Chakra

Bring bright Blue Colour into your life. Wear blue clothing and jewellery. Use bright blue towels. Place blue flowers in your living room.

Find your voice through vocalisation and the use of m*antras*

Take the time to sing or play a musical instrument

Look up at the open sky

Try to find the right words to express your thoughts and feelings

Take voice training or a course in public speaking course

Learn another language

Third Eye Chakra

Ailments

Migraine

Disorders of eye

Hearing impairments

Sinus problems

Headache

Brain diseases

Neurological disorders

Mental illnesses

Check up

If you often have the feeling that life is meaningless and barren

If you regularly suffer from anxiety or depression

If you can't find your way, find it hard to get oriented, or don't perceive your path and purpose in life

If you have a hard time concentrating and your thoughts seem scattered

If you can't hear your inner voice or hear it faintly

If you want to bring more light into your life and you are striving for a higher realisation

Activating the Third Eye Chakra

Read philosophical and spiritual literature

Maintain your dream journal to interpret your own dreams

Meditate under the stars

Let your fantasies take wings because everything that promotes your fantasy, also awakens your *Third Eye Chakra*.

Prefer dark blue clothes.

The best time to work on the *Third Eye Chakra* is during the phase of the wanning moon.

Crown Chakra

Ailments: Weaknesses in the immune system, Nervous Conditions, Paralysis, Mental Illness, Depressions is and Sleep Disorders, Forgetfulness, etc.

Check up

If you believe that there is no life after death

If you wish to experience the mystery and strength of silence

If you feel tired and worn out even though you sleep deeply

If you find no avenue to higher levels of being

If you often feel depressed and lack of joy in life

Activating the Crown Chakra

Open yourself to the power of silence. Practise relaxation.

Enjoy mountain climbing.

Wear white and purple clothing.

Decorate your house with white or purple flowers

The best time to undertake these practices is during the phase of the new moon.

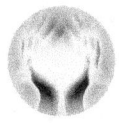

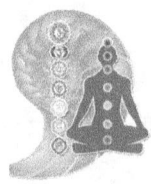

LESSON 6

Hand Positions for Healing Self and Others

In Reiki, it is not the hand positions that heals but the position of your heart.

Important : While placing your hands on each part the following points are to be kept in mind.

1. **Touch — Karma Yoga (Yoga of Action)** — Action and Meditation
2. **Feeling — Bhakti Yoga (Yoga of Love)** — Feeling and Meditation
3. **Attention — Gyan Yoga (Yoga of knowing)** — Knowledge and Meditation (What you give attention to, grows)
4. **Intention of Energy Flowing — Urja Yoga (Yoga of Energy)** — Energy and Meditation
5. **Smiling & Visualising — Haasya Yoga (Yoga of laughter)** — Laughter and Meditation

Note :

In all these types of meditation, *the art of witnessing is the focal point. These five can lead you to witnessing consciousness.* In your journey from the body to mind, the mind to the soul and then to the source. *The whole journey is from visible to invisible.* Reiki can be applied with the hands on, hand off or a combination of both.

Spiritual Guides and Helpers

It is extremely empowering to begin a session with a prayer, calling in God, spiritual guides, teachers and spiritual healers to assist in healing sessions. Also ask the presence of guides of the person receiving the healing.

Self-Healing Hand Positions

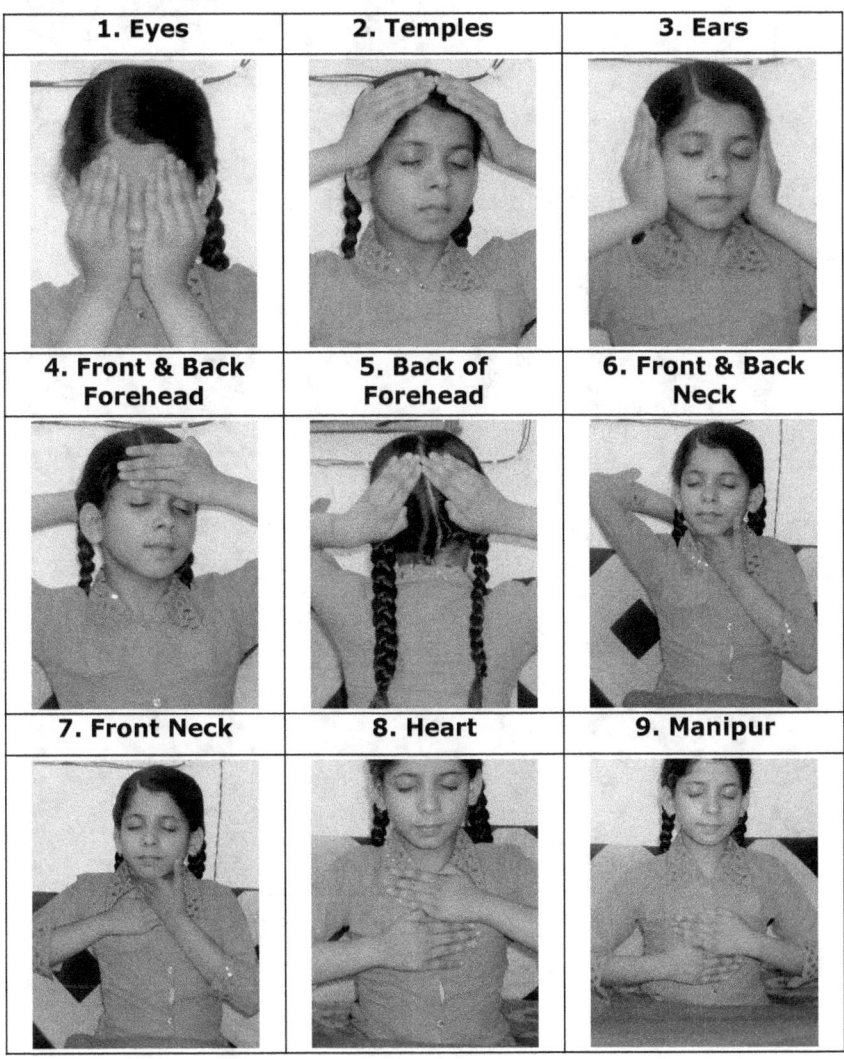

1. Eyes	2. Temples	3. Ears
4. Front & Back Forehead	5. Back of Forehead	6. Front & Back Neck
7. Front Neck	8. Heart	9. Manipur

10. Liver (Right of Stomach)	11. Lung Tips	12. Pancreas & Spleen (Left of Stomach)
13. Swadhisthan (Sacral)	14. Mooladhara (Root)	15. Knees
16. Ankles	17. Soles of feet	18. Shoulders

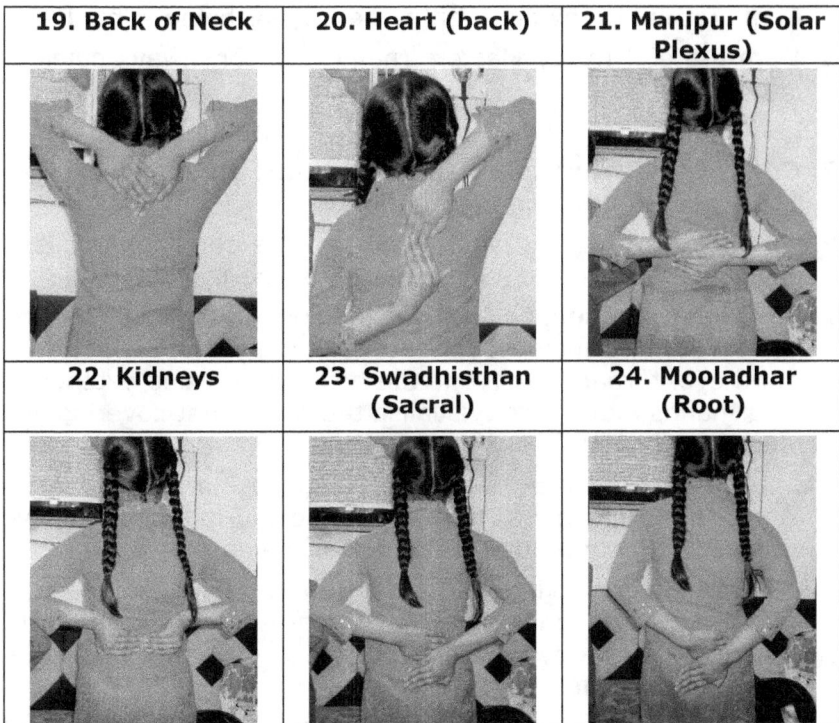

Process for Treating Others

1. **Prepare the room:** Clean the room, burn incense, play soft music, etc
2. **Talk to the patient:** Explain Reiki in a friendly way and learn about the patient's problems
3. **Prepare yourself:** Clean the body and mind and remember that you are always an instrument
4. **Prepare the patient:** Ask the patient to remove his or her wallet, wristwatch, rings and other accessories
5. **Invocation:** Raise your hands with palms facing upward three times to invoke the divine energy and bringing them back to the heart centre. Always remember that the source and its energy are the same and cannot be separated.
6. **Protect yourself:** To ensure protection, you might need to imagine yourself inside a white bubble of light and then ask three times for the best energy to come to you.
7. **Attitude of gratitude**

1. I am grateful to myself (name ....) for being here.
2. I am grateful to the cosmic energy, Reiki for being here.

3. I am grateful to my parents (name ....) for being in my life.
4. I am grateful to my Masters (name ....) for always being in my life.
5. I am grateful to the patient (name ....) for being here.

8. Comb the aura: Loosen and cleanse the etheric aura on all sides of the body from top to toe.

9. Loving contact: lay your hands on the shoulder to make loving contact and to feel the person's energy.

10. Visualise the white light : Imagine white light (healing energy) is just above your head, entering your *crown chakra,* third eye, *throat chakra* and the *heart chakra* and extends to your hands and palms. Visualise the white light covering you and your patient.

11. Begin the healing session: Hand positions for treating others are the same as for treating the self-mentioned above subject to minor adjustments for Convenience.

12. Spiral: Before asking your patient to turn back, you need to do spiralling to connect the Reiki energy given on the front body to the energy you are about to give on the back. The technique is as follows :

The index and middle finger pointed, rest of the fingers folded in the palms. Point the two fingers on the right shoulder in small anticlockwise motions and slowly move towards the shoulders.

Move the fingers towards the tip of the right hand and finish off by flicking at the end of the hand.

Start again from the right shoulder and finish with flicking at the end of the feet.

Start again this time from the left shoulder and finish off flicking at the end of the hands and feet.

Now ask your patient to turn over to the back position.

13. Smooth aura: Place both of your hands three inches above the toes and feel the Reiki energies. Move both the hands towards the top of the head. From the head, slide down both the hands to the toes and neutralise the energies by clapping both the hands or washing them in cold water or salt water.

14. Beam: Step back from your patient to a distance of about six feet. Imagine powerful, laser like beams of milky white Reiki energy emanating from your heart, solar plexus and palms and enveloping your patient's entire body. Imagine that you can direct these beams by moving your eyes.

15. **Seal the healing:** Pray to Reiki to seal the healing you have just provided with Reiki, love and wisdom.
16. **Reiki Finish: Stroking technique or sweeping:** Place three fingers at the top of the neck and draw your hands to the *root chakra* in one quick motion. Do it three times. Now do the same stroke, starting at the top of the neck until the back of the heart and gently press down. (For diabetic patient, sweep the energy up the spine, i.e., in the opposite direction)

Caressing technique or distributing the energy:

Start at the base of the neck, cross the palms at the centre of the back and complete the 8 formation at the base of the spine up to starting point.

17. Closing:

Place your hands in the *Heart Chakra* and mentally say this affirmation.

1. .... (the patient's name) is healed whole and complete.
2. He/she is happy, healthy, harmonious, successful, prosperous, spiritual and blessed with abundance.
3. Thank you Reiki. Thy will be done in full faith and gratitude.

Interpreting the sensations that arise

There may be sensations of heat, cold, flowing, vibrating, trembling, magnetism, static electricity, tingling, colour, sound, pain moving through the healer's hands, etc. A healer may feel as if her/his hands have gone to sleep with a *pin and needle sensation.*

Warmth of intense heat is the most common sensation. This indicates the patient's need for vitality.

- Tingling is often associated with some kind of inflammation.
- Coldness stems from a hidden or forgotten psychological pain that will not allow the organ in question to participate freely in the energy interactions now taking place in the body.
- Magnetic repulsion also points towards blocks in the energy field but normally relates to some vital bodily process.
- Magnetic pull indicates the organ's hunger for Reiki energy.
- Subdued pain is a sign of a blockage getting ready to release.

Instant Reiki

Ask the person who will receive to sit with both feet on the ground.

> - Say your attitude of gratitude.
> - Loosen the etheric aura on all sides of the body from top to toe.
> - Feel the smoothen down aura.
> - Lay your hands on the shoulder to make loving contact and feel the person's energy.
> - Both hands at the crown chakra.
> - One hand on the forehand, the other on the back.
> - One hand on the front of the throat, the other on the back.
> - One hand on the front of the heart, the other on the back.
> - One hand on the front of the solar plexus, the other on the back.
> - One hand on front of the hara, the other on the back.
> - One hand on front of the genitals and the other on the back.
> - Both hands on left and right ankles and feet.
> - Smooth aura.
> - Closing attitude of gratitude.

If the person is in shock, on very stressed, then add one *position either after the heart chakra* position or at the end.

Place one hand on the back of the *heart chakra* and the other in the front of the *solar plexus.*

LESSON 7

Short, Group Treatments & Chakra Balancing

Treatments

For any disease, a minimum of three full body treatments on three consecutive days is essential. After three days, short treatments can be given as follows:

Short Treatment

Three minutes, each on position nos. 2, 3 and 4 on the head and points 8, 9. This will take 15 minutes. After this give Reiki for 10 minutes at the trouble area. *Hence, a short treatment will take 25 minutes.*

Group Treatments

Reiki can be given to a person by a group of Reiki channels or healers. This helps in reducing the time, required to impart a full body treatment. Given below are some body positions to be treated by each healer in a group treatment situation.

(All point numbers in brackets are to be treated for 6 minutes).

Case 1 : (2 persons treating) 39 minutes

1st person: Head end and Right side of the patient Point Nos. 1 to 7, (10), 18, 19 (20)

2nd person: Left side of the patient Point Nos. 8, 9, 11 to 17, 21 to 24

Case 2: (3 persons treating) 27 minutes

1st person: Head end points 1 to 6, 18 and (19)

2nd person: Right side of the patient Points 7 to (11), 20, (21)

3rd person: Left side of the patient Points 12 to 17, 22 to 24

Case 3: (4 persons treating) 21 minutes

1st person: Head end points 1 to 5, (18)

2nd person: Right side of the patient Point 8 to 10, (13), 19 and 20
3rd person: Left side of the patient Point 6, 7, 11, (12), 21 and 22
4th person: Along the legs Point 14, (15) to 17, 23 and 24

There is a great scope for variations in the number and sequence of positions used for the whole body treatment. It will depend greatly upon the practitioner and what is felt to be best for the recipient but no one sequence can be deemed the best one for all.

Chakra Balancing

1. For 21 days, give full body treatment to yourself (all 24 points), each point—3 minutes minimum. This can be done in two or three sittings. The intention is to continue with Reiki also after the first three weeks, but never make Reiki a compulsory drag.
2. If you can continue full body treatment for ever, that is much better. If you cannot do full body then do *Chakra Balancing* following any one of the two methods given below:

Method No. 1 (15 minutes)

1. One palm on forehead, the other palm on the M*uladhara Chakra (Root Chakra)*
2. After 3 minutes, move the lower palm from the *Muladhara* area to *navel* area *(Swadhisthan Chakra)*
3. After 3 minutes, move the lower palm from below the navel area to above the navel the area *(Manipur Chakra)*
4. After 3 minutes, move the lower palm from above the navel area to above the *Heart Chakra (Anahat Chakra)*
5. After 3 minutes, move the lower palm to the neck area *(Vishuddha Chakra)*

So in 15 minutes, the forehead gets 15 minutes energy and other *Chakras* get energy for 3 minutes each.

Method No. 2 (15 minutes)

The following pair of *chakras* are to be balanced in this sequence keeping in mind the intention that you are balancing the particular pair of *chakras:*

1. One *(left)* palm on forehead, the other *(right)* palm on the *Root Chakra* for 5 minutes.

2. Next after 5 minutes, move the (left) upper palm to the Throat Chakra and the lower (right) palm to the Sacral Chakra (above the navel area) without disconnecting your touch.
3. Next after 5 minutes, move the upper (left) palm to the Heart and lower (right) palm over Solar Plexus Chakra.

So, in 15 minutes all the *6 chakras* get 5 minutes energy. The time can be reduced further to 3 minutes minimum.

Chakra Meditation

- Sit in a comfortable position.
- Center yourself. Breathe in deeply, more deeply up to your Root Chakra.
- See red colour surrounding this chakra.
- The root chakra is expanding east to West and North to South.
- Now mentally add the "LAM" vibration and meditate.
- Now look at the Crown Chakra.
- Breathe in a Golden Colour light.
- See the Golden Colour surrounding this Chakra.
- The Crown Chakra in expanding East to West and North to South.
- Now Mentally add the vibration "AUM" while you are concentrating on the ground.
- Look at the Heart Chakra.
- Breathe in a Light Green Colour.
- See the light Green Colour surrounding this Chakra.
- The Heart Chakra is expanding East to West and North to South and meditate with "HUM" vibration.
- Now look at the Third Eye Chakra.
- Breathe in Indigo Colour.
- See the Indigo Colour surrounding this Chakra.
- The Third Eye Chakra is expanding East to West and North to South and meditate with "UM"
- Now look at the Sacral Chakra.
- Breathe in bright Orange Colour.
- See the bright orange colour surrounding this chakra.
- The Sacral Chakra is expanding East to West and North to South and meditate with "VAM"
- Now look at the Throat Chakra.
- Breathe in light blue colour.
- See the light blue colour surrounding this chakra.
- The Throat Chakra is expanding East to West and North to South and meditate with "HUM"
- Now look at the Solar Plexus Chakra.

- Breathe in a muddy yellow colour surrounding this chakra.
- The Solar Plexus Chakra is expanding East to West and North to South and meditate with "RAM" vibration.
- Visualize now a pillar that has been formed from your root chakra to your crown chakra.
- Sit in this pillar devoid of any thoughts and meditate on your Self.

Random Tips

1. **Contracting the Hui Yin**: At your perineum (the space between the genitals and anus) is a Chinese energy point called Hui Yin. To preserve more energy in your body and thus increase the level of Reiki energy follow these two tips :
   a. *Squeeze you Hui Yin.* When you squeeze your perineum, you will feel a stronger sense of energy in your palms.
   b. *Keep your tongue on the palate of your mouth.*
2. **Energy is always neutral.** So remember it is your intention that works the power of intention is very important in Reiki (May Reiki flow for healing). An important point about Reiki is that it is never sent. There is no doing involved. It is always drawn through channel. Drop your attachment or identification as doer.
3. **Energy is one.** Physical, mental, intellectual, spiritual and even sexual are also interrelated.
4. There is difference of energy field by each side of the body. In general the left side is thought to hold female energy while the right side hold the male energy.
5. the energy field produced by the heart is far more powerful than any one thought. Heart electromagnetic field is as much as 5000 times stronger than the field generated by your brain. Many of your so called mental problems like stress, frustration, anger, anxiety and depression are not the problems of the mind at all. They are the problems of emotional centre of the heart.

Qualities of a good healer

These qualities enhance a healer's ability to create rapport and assist in the healing process.
1. Patience, trust and faith.
2. The ability to observe details about someone's body—skin colour, skin temperature, posture, self-image, level of self esteem, etc.

3. The healer as a catalyst—Frequently, a person requiring healing is simply low on energy, which greatly reduces their own ability to move the negative energy out of their body. The healer is present to encourage and assist the recipient to be open and allow the healing to occur.
4. Centering/Grounding — It is very important for anyone working with healing energy to remain centered and grounded.
5. Judgement and criticism: A healer should avoid judgement and criticism.
6. Unconditional love
7. Acceptance: It is very important for the healer to accept everything the is told to him.
8. Non—attachment to results: The healer should remain unattached to a specific outcome.
9. Intuition: The inner guidance may come in the form of feeling a picture or a voice. So a healer should respect his inner guidance.
10. Asking permission: Asking permission helps to create a self open and trusting relationship between the healer and the person being worked with.
11. Feelings: There is saying in healing profession that you can not heal what you cannot feel.
12. Encouraging a person to trust, feel and talk.
13. Surrendering and letting go: Healing is a process of letting go, surrendering, fully feeling and releasing all pain, fears and blockages.

What a Healer Must Avoid
- A healer must avoid loosing temper.
- A healer must avoid every emotional involvement with the patient. His undue attachment may delay the healing process of the patient.
- A healer must avoid irresponsible comments and judgements.
- He has to be a witness and not a judge.
- A healer must avoid using intentions irresponsibly.
- A healer must avoid negative assertive statements as his power may make them true and then he may repent later.
- A healer must always remember that Reiki is not a tool in his hands rather he is tool for this divine energy. He must approach it with inner gratitude.

- A healer is a person who can make a positive difference in the life of others just by his being and his presence.
- He must always remember that Reiki is not Ego based pursuit. Reiki is an expression of unconditional love.

How to Treat

- First create an environment as quite, comfortable and soothing as possible for treatment.
- In the home, set aside a room or designate a small area to be regularly used for client treatment. This "Reiki Space" will become familiar (and thus psychologically comfortable) for clients that require successive treatments and also becomes charged with the nature of Reiki itself, thereby facilitating the healing experience.
- Wear comfortable clothing that won't interfere with the treatment positions.
- For male patients: Remove glasses, vest, jacket, tie and belt, shoes, have his pockets emptied.
- For female patients: Remove glasses, shoes, belt, scarves, jewellry around neck, no girdles or tight pantyhose.
- No terribly snug pants in either case.
- Most treatments by first degree practitioners are hands-on. Remote, or absentee healing is taught in second-degree Reiki.
- However, occasionally it may not be possible to touch the patient directly due to severe skin infection or second/third degree burns, or thick layers of clothing or plaster cast. Or you may wish to treat an infant and don't want to disturb his shallow sleep.
- Know that Reiki finish does require direct physical contact with the skin, though.
- Insist on proper hygiene for yourself, just as you would expect from any medical professional.
- Always have clean hands, washing with soap before treatment and afterwards for 20-30 seconds in cool running water to break the energy flow. If in an emergency water in not available, form the hands in prayer position with fingertips together and press firmly for 30 seconds.
- Place a box of tissues and a sheet or blanket within easy reach.
- The tissues are for eye treatment and certain ailments; the covers for the clients comfort.
- Have the client lie down, if possible, so gravity can aid in pulling Reiki in his body.

- Place a pillow under his head; another under his knees to relieve pressure on the lower back. Employ the sheet or light blanket if the client complains of chills.
- And don't neglect to ensure your own needs either. Remember the comfort of yourself and the client is the next most important thing to Reiki itself during a treatment.
- Make sure the client's feet are not crossed; this tends to short circuit the energy flow.
- Tell the client he may feel worse after the first or second treatment, either due to severe imbalance in an organ (or the body generally) or because you may stop treatment just as the illness has been brought back from the chronic stage before eventual stage.
- If it happens, a minimum three, preferably four consecutive daily treatments will be required unless healing takes place after the first or second treatment.
- "The disease may return from where it came." is a basic Reiki tenet.
- Ask the client about ailments irritated by touching; also inquire about any major surgery.
- Notify people what you are going to do, so you don't scare them to death.
- Treat Head, Front and Back and hold anything that hurts and anything can't go wrong.
- Keep your fingers together, otherwise energy is scattered. Curve the fingers just slightly to rest upon the contours of the body rather than making them stiff and flat.
- Imagine you are going to touch your lover in a gentle embrace and you will get it just perfect.
- Begin by spending 8-10 minutes on each position.
- As you practice Reiki and your bio-sensory system becomes more attuned to the universal life energy, you will sense a varying rhythmic rise and fall of energy under your hands. Your power to
- channel Reiki will also increase, and the treatment time will shorten.
- Extremely diseased centers will probably need prolonged placements.
- Whatever your hands will tell you through its sinusoidal pattern when to break, do so at the end of the cycle of peak-to ebb flow just as the energy is about to rise again. That completes one energy cycle for that particular organ of the body drawing in the most Reiki.
- Each period will differ, depending on the organ and its condition.

- If the client has organs missing due to surgery, treat as if they are present anyway. Reiki can help set up energy pattern, within the body to balance the body as if that organ were physically present and will release adhesions if they exist.
- A cold spot indicates a dysfunctioning organ or impaired circulation. Hold the area until warm.
- There is no such thing as a partial treatment because the body is all linked in, as you all know.
- For instance, if a person has diabetic blindness you are not going to cure the eyes until you cure the pancreas, because the pancreas is what manufactures insulin and a lack of insulin is what creates diabetes and diabetes is what can create diabetic blindness, etc. So until the pancreas is healed nothing is going to happen to diabetic blindness.
- So aside from emergency situations, always give the whole body treatment before focusing on particular ailments for additional Reiki. As you going of your time, the client should be equally agreeable to give of his time for a particular treatment. The client has given you the authority by requesting a Reiki treatment, so be firm about what you know must be done.
- If partial treatment must be done, treat the solar plexus and adrenals.(This is good for energy revitalization and bringing things back to life)
- Reiki is pulled through the body at a rate corresponding to the need of the client.
- The more energy needed to regenerate, rejuvenate and revitalize the injured body, the longer the healing will generally take.
- At the end of 10 minutes almost every organ has all the Reiki it needs.
- Always remember energy follows desire and thoughts. Where ever we direct our desires and thoughts, energy flows in that direction.

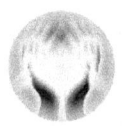

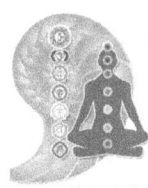

Emotions & Their Locations in the Body

Hands
Giving and receiving
Holding on the reality
Reaching goals
Fear of action

Arms
Express the heart centre, love
Enables us to move and connect in the external world

Forearm
Means of attaining goals
Fear of inferiority

Upper arm
Strength to act
Fear of being discouraged

Elbow
Connects the strength of arms to the action of the forearm

Shoulders
Where we carry the weight of the world
Fear of responsibility
Women store a lot here

Upper back

(Particularly between the two shoulder blades) we carry strong anger

Back
Where we store all of our unconscious emotions and excess tension

Lower back
Junction between lower and upper body movement
Men store a lot here due to the storing of emotions in the belly

Pelvis
Seat of Kundalini energy
Root of basic survival, needs and actions

Gluteus muscles
Holding in emotions not releasing and letting to anal blockage

Hamstrings
Self-control issue
Letting go

Abductor
Inner thigh
Contain sexually charged issues

Lower leg
enables movement towards goals
fear of action

Ankles
Create balance

Nose
Related to the heart (coloration and bulbousness)
sense and smell, sexual response
self-recognition

Eyes
Show how we see the world
Nearsighted is more withdrawn
Farsighted is less inner-oriented
Windows of the soul

Mouth
Survival issue
How we take in nourishment security
Capacity to take in new ideas

Brow
Intuitive centre
Emotional expression

Forehead
Intellectual expression

Ears
Our capacity to hear
Have acupuncture points for every area of the body

Neck
Thought and emotions come together
Stiffness is due to withheld statements

Jaw
Tension indicates blockage of emotional and verbal communication
Fear of ease of expression

Arms and hands
Are extensions of the heart centre
Express love and emotion

Chest
Relationship issue
Heart and love emotions
Respiration and circulation

Solar Plexus (Diaphragm)
Power issues
Emotional control issues—power wisdom centre

Abdomen
Seat of the emotions
Contains our deepest feelings
Centre of sexuality
Digestive System

Genitals
Related to root *chakra* containing *Kundalini*
Survival issues
Fear of life

Thigh
Personal strength
Trust in one's own abilities
Fear of inadequate strength

Knees
Fear of death
Fear of death of the old-self or ego
Fear of change

Feet
Show if we are grounded
Connected with reaching our goals
Fear of completion

Face
Express the various "masks" of our personality
Shows how we "face" the world.

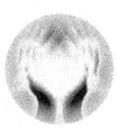

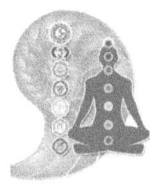

LESSON 9

Treating Common Ailments with Reiki

"Every adversity, every failure, every heartache carries with it the seed of an equal or greater benefit. ~ Napoleon Hill

1. Allergy, Bronchitis, Fever: Whole body
2. Skin disease
3. Anaemia: Whole body, Liver and Pancreas
4. Anger, Acidity, Restlessness: *Manipur Chakra*
5. Arthritis: Knees, Kidneys and Affected Area
6. Asthma: Throat, Lung tips and Heart
7. Backache: Manipur, Swadhisthan, Root Chakra and complete Back portion
8. Chest pain: Swadhisthan and Chest
9. Broken bone: Affected area
10. Boils, inflammation: Affected area
11. Cancer: Whole body and affected area
12. Cough and Cold: Throat, Heart, Manipur Lungs and Forehead
13. Cramps: Swadhisthan front and back and affected area
14. Diabetes: Pancreas and Liver
15. Drug addiction: Whole body and *heart chakra*
16. Ear ailments: Ear
17. Fits: Point Nos 1-6 and Manipur
18. Eye ailments: Point Nos. 1,2 and 5
19. Food Poisoning: Heart, Manipur, Swadhithan, Point Nos. 20 and 23
20. Female genital disorders: *Swadhisthan Chakra* and Ovary
21. Hands and Shoulder pain: Affected area and *Heart Chakra*
22. Gastric and Constipation: Liver and Pancreas, Swadhisthan and Manipur

23. Headache, Head injury: Point Nos. 1-6
24. Heart Problems: Manipur, Swadhithan and *Heart Chakra*
25. Internal Bleeding: Affected area and *Manipur Chakra*
26. Piles: *Muladhar Chakra*
27. High and Low Blood Pressure: Both sides of Neck, Heart and Swadhisthan Chakra
28. Hair Loss: Point No. 2, Affected area, Head Massage
29. Injury/Wounds: Affected area
30. Leg Problems: *Muladhar Chakra*
31. Mumps: Whole body, *Muladhar,* Throat and Jaws
32. Obesity: Thyroid
33. Paralysis: Whole body thrice a day
34. Parkinson: Whole body, Point No. 1-6
35. Pregnancy: Heart, M*anipur, Swadhisthan, Muladhar and womb*
36. Dislocated Backbone : Whole spine/backbone
37. Spondilitis: Back Neck and the whole back area
38. Tongue related: Soles of feet
39. Tonsils: Point Nos. 1, 2, 3 and Jaws
40. Ulcers: Affected area
41. Concentration: Third Eye
42. Self-confidence and Expression: Throat, Heart and Manipur
43. Depression/Resentment: Manipur, *Swadhisthan* and Knees
44. Memory: Point No. 2 and Both sides of Neck
45. Peace: One hand at Manipur and the other at Swadhisthan
46. Alcohol and Smoking: Upper Lungs, *Heart Chakra,* Liver and Knees
47. Laziness: *Heart Chakra*
48. Self-faith: Thighs
49. Fear: Knees

Reiki Morning Prayer

Make a bow to the Sun two times.
    (In your heart, say two times, "Thanks to the God")
    Clap your hands two times.
    (Purify the space around you)

Say the Prayer three times
HARAI TAMAE (Cleanse all)
KIYOME TAMAE (Purify all)
MAMORI TAMAE (Protect all)
SACHI-HAE-TAMAE (Make all being happy)
A-MA-TE-RA-SU-OO-MI-KAMI (the Sun's Mantra)
Wish, if you have.
Say three times
KAMNAGARA TAMASHI HAEMASE
(as the God wishes)
Make a bow to the Sun one time.
(In your heart, say one time, "Thanks to the God")

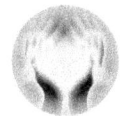

LESSON 10

Other Energy Exercises

Aura Cleansing Methods

Practise daily *auric cleansing*. After all, we wash our bodies everyday. So once we realise that our auras are energetic extensions of our bodies, it makes sense to cleanse them too. Some cleaning methods are as under:

1. Singing Bowl

Sounds have a great cleansing property. That is why bells were rung during religious and sacred ceremonies. Likewise, cleanse your aura using a singing bowl.

2. Crystals

Specific crystals may also be used in cleansing.

3. Salt Bath

4. Bach Flower Remedies

There are 38 Different bach flower remedies. Several flower remedies are effective in auric cleansing. *Crab apple* is the best for your aura cleansing.

5. Auric Brushing

Use your hands to brush your aura and then dispose off the negative energy.

Get into the habit of scanning your aura on a regular basis and learn strengthening your aura. *Change your aura, change your life. Realise the healing power of aura.*

6. Smudging : How to do it

Smudging is a way of using the smoke from burning herbs as a way to cleanse the body, and object or a given area of negative influences. Use *smudging* to cleanse crystals and use it also for protecting your room or home from bad vibe producing events. The three most used plant materials for smudging are 1. sage of all types 2. cedar and 3. sweet grass.

7. Reiki and Guided Imagery

Imagination is a potent healer that has long been overlooked by the practitioners. Imagery can relieve pain, speed healing and help the body subdue hundred of ailments. The power of the mind to influence the body is quite remarkable. Imagery is the most fundamental language. *Everything you do the mind processes through images.* When we recall events from our past or childhood, we think of pictures, images, sounds, pain, etc. It is hardly ever be through words. Images are not necessarily be limited to visual-but can be sounds, tastes, smells. Imagery is the language that the mind uses to communicate with the body. Imagery is the biological connection between the mind and the body. This is also extremely useful in mind-body healing. In Reiki, visualisation and imagery are very useful in healing as well. A good affirmation according to Covey must have *five basic ingredients:*

1. It is personal
2. It is present tense
3. It is emotional
4. It is positive
5. It is visual

Laws of Cure

There are *three laws of cure.* They are :

1. A remedy starts from the top of the body and works downwards.
2. A remedy works from within the body outward and from major to minor organs.
3. Symptoms clear in reverse order of appearance.

Application of three principles of cure means that you will feel better emotionally before you will feel better physiologically.

The Power of Asking

There is a power inside you that is beyond anything that you have yet imagined. You have the ability to manifest anything that you want with pure love and effortless ease. There is no limit on what you can create into your life. *You are unlimited, unbounded, pure potential energy.* You can consciously attract any experience you want at any time. Yet when you are super specific about what you want and ask from a surrendered place that is free from lack, you are one step closer to becoming a manifesting master in *Reiki*. Remember people who ask confidently get more than those who are hesitant and uncertain. You should not send out desperate and needy energy into the universe. This panic shuts down your ability to receive. So the true energetic detachment is very very necessary in Reiki and you should transcend the needy grasping mind.

Moving and directing the energy flow

There are three commonly used methods for energy movement and flow.

1. **Inflated Balloon:** Have the person focus on placing the issue they wish to heal into the balloon. Then let them blow these issues into the balloon filling it as full as possible. Have them hold the balloon next to their body over the effected area. Next with their eyes shut, have the person visualise all their emotions as—pain, anger, hurt and frustrations—into the balloon. After they have placed all of this in the balloon, tell them that they can release and heal this issue and the related emotions by breaking the balloon.

2. **Energy Ball:** A variation of above technique is to have person, with their eyes shut, focus their mind and visualize the energy of their issue or illness. Ask them to gather all of the energy associated with it and to push it out of their body until it is about 12 inches in front of their forehead. Then ask them to compress this energy into a tight ball. After they have done this, ask them again if all of the energy associated with it is out of their body and inside the energy ball. When they say that all of the energy is out of the body, ask them to focus their mind on the energy ball and compress it even tighter. Clap your hand as loudly as you can in the area of energy ball and visualize that energy ball is completely released or greatly reduced.

3. **Clapping:** Another technique is to have the person shut their eyes and focus on the issue. Watch until you can see they have focussed intensely on the issue. Then, when least expected, clap your hand as loud as you can in the area of the blockage. This shatters the negative energy.

LESSON 11

Advanced Reiki

1. Reiki Symbols

There are three kinds of symbols or viewpoints about symbols that are used in healing, meditation and for spiritual, mental and emotional development. One view is that symbols like the forms used in sacred geometry or the tattwas and Yantra Mandal the actual shape or form contains the power to waken an ability or create a result or convey mystical information and realisation itself.

Another possibility is that symbols acquire power by being charged with the intention of people or from being in proximity to spiritual ability or teachers or places or from repeated use. The third kind of symbol or view of symbols is that they are tools or triggers that enable you to connect with and use a spiritual function, information, and so forth. The power exists separate from the symbol itself. The symbol is more like an on button. The power is in what the symbols represent rather than having any power of its own.

Symbols are a tool to help you connect with and focus and use the Reiki energy. You may not need to consciously use them constantly when you are more experienced. In the beginning it is quite sensible to use them, in time you may just tune in to the Reiki functions.

On the other hand many people do always use the symbols every time they use Reiki neither way is better than the other way.

In the Reiki symbols, the intent and the active force coincide, not in the air or on paper, but in your heart, soul, mind, spirit. If the intent isn't there, you might just as well not draw anything. Contrary to the popular story of symbols appearing in bubbles, Usui Sensei apparently may have started teaching his Reiki without them and later introduced the symbols to help provide focus for people who don't sense the energy as easily as others.

As a Practitioner, you will know if the active use of the symbols becomes optional for you. It is best to continue to be open to learn as much as possible about the deeper meanings behind these terms or symbol forms. It does not mean that working without symbols is "more advanced" than working with them. It is simply different, not better or more advanced, and that what is true or right for one person may not be the best way for another person.

Even if you do not need to draw the symbols to activate Reiki it can be valuable to study them and use them in meditation.

Level Two-Reiki Symbols

In second degree Reiki, you will learn the following three symbols,
1. *The Power Symbol*
2. *The Mental Symbol*
3. *The Distant Healing Symbol*

The Symbols are traditionally drawn mentally or with the whole hand while repeating the name /mantra of the symbol silently either one or three times depending on the "school" your teacher belongs to. They can be visualized whole and "thrown", drawn with the whole hand or with the third eye using tiny head movements, or drawn with the tongue on the roof of the mouth.

For room clearing and blessing some practitioners use both hands held palms together as in the Gassho or prayer position to draw large symbols with very sweeping motions of the arms. Some people draw the symbol only at the beginning of treatment others draw them each time they change hand placements. Some people draw all the symbols every time and others only draw the one or ones they are calling on.

Most students find that it becomes much easier to memorize and draw the symbols after they have been attuned to Reiki than it is before the attunement.

1. The Power Symbol - CHO KU REI

(Cho koo ray) (long o in Cho) is the Usui power boost mantra and symbol to increase the effect of Reiki. This function is said to call in higher universal energy and accelerates Reiki from low to high and gives greater focus to the energy. Power boost is used with the other energies as well as by itself during all treatments hands on or distance.

This energy has been used to clear rooms and crystals and to charge food and water, and in manifestation procedures. This symbol has been used as a sort of Good Luck charm or "blessing pump" and as a protective sign. The symbol shown is with the counter clockwise spiral which is the traditional direction.

The *Cho Ku Rei* symbol can help start *Reiki* flowing or give it a feeling of being more finely tuned or powerful. Most practitioners use it at the beginning of sessions by drawing it on the palms of their hands, drawing it with the third eye or with the tongue on the roof of their mouth or by mentally visualising the symbol on or over the body or the person being treated.

This Reiki function is used for activating and enhancing energy, focussing, stabilising and fixing the energy for clearing, cleansing, recharging, revitaliing and general healing. It is also used for improving the physical or material energy state. This function helps align human energy with the natural rhythms of The Earth.

The first symbol is often called *Focus* or *Power* symbol or *Booster*. The *Cho Ku Rei* is sometimes nicknamed "the light switch" as it connects us to the energy, like a light switch being turned on. It is thought to turn up the energy, and opens us as channels of the Reiki energy. It can help overcome negative resistance patterns. It can help reduce pain.

Cho Ku Rei is also used in space clearing. To cleanse a room, draw or visualise *Cho Ku Rei* in the corners or on the walls, floor and ceiling of a room. While intending that the room be cleansed and filled with energies of love and compassion. Mentally throw Cho Ku Rei into the room while intending the room be filled with light. Many people do this in the treatment area before doing treatments or Attunements.

Draw *Cho Ku Rei* on objects in your environment while you intend that they be cleansed and operate for your highest good. Draw the symbol on objects and run Reiki into them to charge them with Reiki. *Cho Ku Rei* can be used in almost as many ways as you can think up.

You can use the *Cho Ku Rei* at the start of a healing session to feel the energetic connection to the Reiki source. You can use it to focus power at each hand position and on any problem areas. You could draw it over the person at the end of a healing session to seal and stabilise the healing.

Some people also use *Cho Ku Rei* for protection. For protection, draw the symbol on a piece of paper and place it on or under things, you want filled with Reiki or mentally visualise or invoke it. You can visualise or imagine the Symbol surrounding you. Draw the symbol in front and in back over and on both sides of yourself. Draw it over food and water before you eat and drink. You can also visualise or draw it over your head before meditation or meditate on the symbols themselves.

Draw the *Cho Ku Rei* on the shower head prior to taking a shower so that the water is filled with Reiki as it cleanses you. Run Reiki into your bath water.

To use *Cho Ku Rei* for manifestation, you can activate Cho Ku Rei and clearly visualise what you intend to manifest while running Reiki. This will not bring you things that are not in accord with your high self and soul purpose. Experiment! When doing any manifestation procedure, you must focus on the positive form of your intended manifestation.

After cleansing, the crystals you can use the power symbol to empower them instead of a generator crystal, especially if you use crystals a lot on grids for doing multiple sends. This is different than traditional crystal clearing and charging methods. Always meditate to confirm that the work you wish to do with the crystal is in accord with the natural purpose and desire of the Crystal.

When you find your energy flagging and have little time for a self-treatment, draw the power symbol down your body and give yourself a 5-minute zap.

Draw it on the palm of each hand before sending distant healing. Draw it into the corners of any rooms that need clearing. Draw it over flower essences, essential oils or shampoo and other personal care items. Draw it on a piece of paper and wrap it around a sick tree to keep the energy working. Draw it over food before cooking and eating.

2. The Mental Symbol - SEI HE KI (SHK)

(SEI HE KI) Harmony, Emotional and Mental Healing *Sei He Ki* is used to facilitate emotional and mental healing and to assist self-programming. It is used when treating addictions and habits as well as all other mental and emotional concerns. it is said to work on the subconscious. Some teachers use it on the first four *chakras* only and some use it on all positions. The mental/emotional healing function helps to balance the right and left sides of the brain. This symbol is often used for healing unwanted habits or for programming in desired habits.

Sei He Ki

Sei He Ki is called the *Harmony symbol.* This symbol is traditionally associated with the moon and emotional cycles. It can help bring emotional release and to reduce stress and restore high spirits. Sei He Ki functions to restore psychological and emotional balance and bring deep healing. It also promotes self-growth by increasing sensitivity and acceptance. Help with understanding relationships, releasing bad habits, and all sorts of disorders and trauma with gentle energy of love and harmony, used for restoring psychological and emotional balance.

It is used to heal mental and emotional habits that no longer work for you, Sei He Ki can help with emotional and mental distress. It is also used to bring up and heal the emotional issues underneath the physical problems. It helps reinforce and support positive behaviour changes.

This function is for healing and releasing those feelings, desires and conditioning that keeps us in negative patterns.

Healing with the SHK can be as simple as using the symbol while doing a healing using the regular hand positions. It can also be used as part of meditations to help release and heal conditioning and patterns that underlie problems.

You can use Sei He Ki to empower your affirmations and resolutions and for working on specific areas where you feel emotional processing is needed. Simply turn on Reiki and activate the Focus and Harmony functions with the intention that Reiki works on the kind of issue you are seeking to heal. Use Sei He Ki for issues with fear, anger, grief or resentment, or to enhance your own ability to love yourself and others or to develop positive qualities, such as for serenity or courage or compassion or zest.

Here are some more uses for the Mental/Emotional symbol. The Sei He Ki.

Use the emotional symbol in the *chakras* with the intent that emotional and mental issues be balanced and healed. if the treatment is specifically for emotional/mental issues), end by wrapping the recipient in Reiki and seal it with the SHK, too. Recipients will often report a feeling of lightness and a lifting of despair and stress. You may want to use the HSZSN too, since many emotional issues have roots from the recipient's past.

If you are feeling 'out of balance' all you have to do is to place your hands on your head and think of the SHK and it will tend to bring you back into balance. This symbol heals more on the higher levels of consciousness, and is thought to work more in the aura field than on the physical body.

If a person is complaining even of a headache often it is coming from some type of emotional or mental tension, so using the SHK symbol is appropriate in dissipating headaches.

The SHK can also be used for getting rid of 'bad vibes' and for protection.

Bad vibes or negativity coming from others or perceived as coming from others exists on a mental and emotional level so that you can use the symbol as a form of psychic protection. What you can do is simply draw this symbol around yourself, perhaps saying something like, "I protect myself now with divine love and wisdom". Use the symbol on each side of you, behind, above, below you and in front of you, and repeat the words. As you do so, you should feel the protective energy begin to develop around you. It will tend to harmonise any negative vibrations that will be coming from others. You can use the SHK and the CKR for spiritual protection. Another way to give yourself protection is to visualise an egg shaped energy field around you with the SHK moving around the surface of the egg, starting at your feet and working its way around the egg and upwards until it reaches the top of your head. Do the same with the CKR. Often at work or even at home we deal with people who we like to think of as our friends but sometimes there are negative feelings that come up and it is very valuable to be able to protect our selves and harmonise the situation by using Reiki.

You can use the SHK to assist with memory. If you have forgotten something, your keys for instance, take a moment and place your hands on top of your head and use SHK there. As you do the Reiki say to yourself 3 times "I will remember where I placed my keys within one minute". Then just relax. Sometimes using Reiki in this way will help you conscious mind to align itself to that memory, causing you to remember just where you placed your keys!!

Worth a try anyway! It can work equally well for other things you have forgotten - a person's name, a telephone no. etc. Often you are trying too hard to remember and the Reiki energy will simply help you to relax so that the information will surface again.

Students can use this symbol when taking tests or exams. Before the test draw the SHK over the paper to help your mind to attune to the correct answers. Of course it goes without saying that you must have studied beforehand! Reiki will help your conscious mind access the correct piece of information from all the data held in your brain. Use it when that extra concentration is needed and you are feeling bored in class. Place your hands on your knees and think of the SHK as you listen to the tutor and it will help you to retain the information being given. Affirmations are a powerful tool when one is trying to achieve goals. You can simply repeat a positive phrase over again in your mind or write it on a piece of paper. Repetition is the key and the SHK can be used to empower your affirmations. In this way they tend to be more deeply embedded in the subconscious mind.

Any time you are having an argument or disagreement, it can be very healthy and valuable to use the SHK. Just imagine the symbol being between you and the person you are having the argument with. It will tend to filter the energy that passes between you, thereby assisting you in creating harmony and peace and understanding.

Emotional Healing Symbol or Self-Treatment

Place your non-dominant hand at the base of the skull and with the dominant hand over the top of your head (palm facing head), sign the power symbol once saying its name three times, then sign the emotional symbol once saying its name three times, then again sign the power symbol once saying its name three times. Then place the signing hand on the top of the head. Now, with both hands remaining on the head, repeat the affirmation for 3-5 minutes, or for a rise and fall of the energy, or as many times as felt necessary. Sample affirmation - "I now have what I need to see the issues in my life in a new way and the wisdom, strength, courage and love to follow through with what is given." You can use whatever affirmation desired so long as it is in the positive (absolutely no negative words as no, not, don't, etc.) and in the present tense.

The Emotional Healing Program

This works on long held emotional constrictions which may or may not manifest as physical abnormalities, bringing them to the surface and releasing them. Where there's a chronic physical condition it's always worth doing this emotional program at the beginning of a treatment.

The symbols used are the Third Symbol, The First Symbol, and the Second Symbol. Included and absolutely necessary to this program are also a visualization and an affirmation.

Self-Healing: Sit down, Calm Yourself and Begin. Connect to the issue as in distance healing. Draw the Third Symbol and see it going into your crown; then draw the First Symbol, again seeing them going into your crown; then draw the Second Symbol, see it going into your crown; then draw the First Symbol again.

Visualisation: Put your hands either on your face or head, whichever is the most comfortable. See your head filling with gold from the symbols and from your hands. When the head has filled the gold spreads to fill the whole body. When the body is completely full the gold then overflow out of the feet. The energy then turns, comes out and up the outside of the body on all sides and into the body again through the Crown Chakra. Continue this visualization - it should look like a sort of elongated torus shape, constantly on the move both inside and outside the body.

Affirmation When the visualization has reached this point add the affirmation: "I send the light, [name], deep into the inner recesses of your mind, bringing light to the darkness, that shadows disappear."

Keep this up for around half an hour or so and then stop. This is a very powerful program. I suggest that you do it for an issue no more than 4 days in a row, then leave it for a month or so and watch for developments before doing it again.

Have your client lie down and follow the above routine. Your hands should be either under their head or curled onto the forehead. You or they may prefer to sit up, in which case your hands should be on the top of their head.

Healing Situations Connect to the situation in the usual way and follow the above routine.

Visualise a ball of light as the situation and then use the affirmation.

This program is amazingly effective at bringing to the surface and releasing hidden emotional issues - so for example, if you (or a client) have been having a lot of accidents you might then send healing to this situation using this program, but would connect to it along the lines of "the issue behind my recent accidents". Watch what happens around you - it may be that the issue is one that you are amazed has any connection.

Releasing emotional and mental blockages anger etc.

Hold your hand palms outward above your throat and heart and visualize or mentally draw the Sei He Ki state your intention to release and remove the blocked energy or negative feeling and then just allow Reiki to run as usual can be used for others as well as self.

Reiki is complimentary and enhances most forms of treatment. On a spiritual level Reiki can be quite valuable and protective but people with serious Psychological conditions should probably seek Reiki treatment from practitioners that have credentials in appropriate fields as well as in Reiki if possible. Use Reiki as a healing for these types of conditions but do not analyze unless you are qualified.

In mental healing Reiki works with the consciousness by transforming negative influence into positive and removing energy blocks. Reiki works on the areas of the mind where we hold our programming, conditioning and the causes of problems and illnesses. A stumbling block in mental healing is the client's belief system itself. If the patient does not want a cure then they will mentally resist healing. This is common in the case of addictions, parental and societal programming where many sessions may be required during which you may get fed up with "failure" or the patient sees little benefit in your healing.

All sessions work to some degree but YOU CAN NOT FORCE HEALING. You can not force your will on others. Just allow Reiki to flow. Do not try to direct it to a specific outcome. Your responsibility is not to do anything that would be dabbling with someone else's mind.

People are often very susceptible to suggestion during treatment you might repeat an affirmation that you and the client have chosen before hand but should be very careful about what you say.

A Process for Reinforcing Positive Change Have the client sit on a comfortable, upright chair.
1. Decide with client on affirmations and positive results required.
2. Place your hands on the shoulders and relax the patient for 1 to 2 minutes Or until Reiki tapers off.

3. Remove one hand, keeping the other in place, and slowly trace Reiki Symbol CHO-KU-REI above but not on cranium while focusing on the mantra (name) of the symbol. Repeat as many times as you feel is needed, although once is generally enough.
4. Replace hand on shoulders for up to 5 more minutes or until Reiki tapers off be aware of any images or information you receive
5. Place your hands on Reiki Head Position (top of head) and relax the client for 1 to 2 minutes.
6. Remove one hand and trace the Reiki Symbol SEI-HI-KI above but not on the cranium while focussing your mind on the *mantra* (name) of the symbol on any affirmations you have agreed on with the client. Repeat as often as you feel is necessary.
7. Replace hands on head and repeat sequence from [1] but substitute SEI-HI-KI for CHO-KU-REI.
8. Finish after 15 to 20 minute session using CHO-KU-REI to end session.

3. The Distant Symbol - HON SHA ZE SHO NEN (HSZSN)
(Hawn Shaw Zay Show Nen)

Hon sha ze sho nen is used for sending Reiki hands off for absentee healing and treating issues from the past including past life issues.

This function also gives you the ability to use all the Reiki functions for hands off treatments at any distance at all. you can use this symbol function long distance and to beam the energies to someone in the room with you. This is especially useful in treating children and animals in treating yourself on areas you can not reach and when in public or anyplace where a hands on treatment might be impractical.

This symbol is the most complicated of the Reiki symbols but can be easy to learn by practising writing it. Start with one stroke, repeat that stroke and add one more, repeat these and add the next one, continue adding a stroke with each drawing this way until you are able to write the entire symbol. Or you may prefer to break it up into several sections and learn one section at a time.

Many people do find that they can activate the Reiki function by direct intention without drawing or visualising the symbol at all. I feel that it does have value to memorise it as well as the others. There are some differences in the way different teachers write this symbol usually one writes it as your teacher did unless you have an intense intuitive call to another style.

Hon Sha Ze Sho Nen (HSZSN): Remote Healing

HSZSN Remote, Distant or absentee symbol is associated with the sun and its life giving energy. This symbol is used for connecting to people, places, ideas, things and situations which are distant in time, place or memory. Often used together with other symbols.

Distant healing can bridge time and space, allowing you to send healing energy across a room, or around the world to heal past wounds and to contribute healing energies for others and in situations such as natural disasters and political crises. You can use HSZSN to treat anxieties you have about events in the future. Some people use it to create healing packages to be tapped into later or sent ahead for a known future need.

Activation of the Symbols

Just drawing symbols will not activate it. To activate each symbol draw the symbol once using your third eye chakra or your index and middle finger, then in your mind say the name of the symbol thrice and say charge, charge, charge. For power symbol beam white light, for mental symbol pink light and for distant healing symbol golden light. Between two symbols it is advisable to wait and let each symbol activate a different level of energy. Go slow and don't be in rush to draw and activate the symbols.

Remote or Distance Healing

There are many ways to do distance healing. When using this symbol the Hon Sha Ze Sho Nen is drawn or visualized at the beginning of treatment just before designating your intended recipient. This function enables us to send healing energies to others at a distance.

This can be used to send Reiki across the street or to other parts of the world. It can be used when doing hands on Reiki healing would be inappropriate (with a burn patient or someone with sexual abuse issues). In these cases Reiki can be sent distantly from across the room or from a few inches or feet away.

Such line of sight use of the distance healing symbol is often called "Beaming". Some people help focus their intent when beaming by imagining the Reiki energy radiating out from their eyes or heart or hands.

Some people like to hold their hands up toward the person or people they are doing the treatment with. Most people find that they can beam or send the remote treatment without raising their hands.

When you heal a problem at its origination point quite often many subsequent problems that are based from that initial event will resolve themselves and heal almost instantly. Used with the emotional healing function you can obtain results that are similar to those obtained in "soul retrieval". or "etheric recovery" Sometimes using the distance function can assist with past life recall.

Some have used this function to send the treatment ahead to a specific point in the future.

The full meaning is not "no past, no present, no future", but more like "Right consciousness is the root of everything", or "integrity can correct all ". Hon Sha Ze Sho Nen is made up out of five separate kanji The way we write this symbol these five characters are compressed into each other. The superficial translation would be something like 1. Originally (in essence, by nature) 2. Person (being. entity) 3. Exactly (right, just) 4. Righteous (certainly, straight path) 5. Mind (presence of the heart, character). The long-term effect is to help us live in the present, free of blocks and worries about the past and future.

2. Nine Ways of Distant Healing

1. Photo Technique

The simplest technique for sending Reiki to someone at a distance is to use a photo of them. Draw the three symbols with your finger on the picture and say the names of each symbol three times as you draw them. Intend that the person be filled with Reiki. Then place the photo between your hands, and then send the Reiki. You can also do a self treatment using the photo under your hands as you treat yourself intending that the person receive the treatment.

2. Writing the Recipient's Name on a Piece of Paper

If you do not have a photograph of the recipient, take a clean piece of paper, write his full name clearly on it and below his name draw the three symbols. Repeat his name thrice and intend to remove his negativity. Then draw the Distant Healing symbol, the Mental symbol and the Power symbol on your palms and activate your Palm chakras.

Hold the paper in your energized left hand. With your third eye chakra or your two fingers draw the Distant healing symbol, the Power symbol and the Mental symbol on the paper photograph with the intention to draw the symbols on him. From your palm chakras, beam Reiki to him. Do a standard Reiki treatment with the intention of healing him. Pray in affirmation and envision him healed and healthy.

Intend to cover him with golden light. To seal the energy within him, draw the Power symbol on him through his name on the paper.

3. The Proxy Methods (Knee Method, Pillow Method, Teddy Bear Method)

Proxy methods are using one thing to represent another. People use these methods to help gain an energetic rappart with the person.

Many people have difficulty believing that Reiki can transcend time and space and the proxy gives their minds something to grasp to get past the limitations of the mind. Anything can be used as a proxy.

Technically, the photo technique above is a proxy method that uses the photo to represent the person.

The basis of the proxy method is that we intend that the object represents the person. If you are using a pillow, you would intend that the top part represent the crown, the middle the waist and the bottom the feet. A teddy bear is easy, the head represents the head, etc. In the knee method, use the right knee and thigh to represent the back and the left knee and thigh to represent the front of the person treated. The knee corresponds to the head, the base of the thigh would be the feet. You can also use your thumb. Assume it as the person and wrap other fingers around it and send Reiki.

Which ever method you use, begin by drawing the three symbols on the object used to represent the person. Then treat the proxy intending that you are treating the person.

4. Finger Method

The finger method is another method of using a representation of the person to send distant Reiki. It is useful if you only have one hand free or in a place where you want to send distance Reiki but do not want to attract attention to yourself. Basically, this procedure uses one of the fingers of one hand to represent a person or situation that you want to send distance healing to. Wrap your fingers of one hand around the finger that you are using as your representation. Intend that you are sending distant Reiki to that person or situation. You can state it out loud as well if you like. As you do Reiki on your finger, you are doing Reiki on the person.

5. Visualisation Technique

Its one way is to visualise the recipient to be standing in front of you. Another method is to imagine that you are there with the person receiving the healing, and do the healing as if you were there. The trick is being able to keep the visual image in your mind while you do the healing. If required, you can use strong visual skills and intent.

6. Beaming Technique

There are two different beaming techniques. They are beaming istantly and in person or beaming to someone in your location. To do distant beaming, draw all three symbols in the air. State the name of the person you wish to heal and any other details about them that you need to feel connected. Intend that the person will receive Reiki as you send. Hold one or both hands at the chest level palms facing outward in front of you. If you use only one hand, place the other comfortably in your lap. Then simply send the Reiki.

In-person beaming is distant Reiki but when you are with the person, it is something you can do when you want to send reiki to someone in the line of sight. This is useful for people with touch issues, or for people who it would be inappropriate to touch like burn victims or those with infectious diseases. To do beaming, extend the palms towards the person and use the symbol/word for distant healing. The difference between this and distant healing is you can see the person.

You can also beam from the body, projecting out from every cell. You can also beam from the eyes.

7. Doing Reiki on a List of Recipients

In this method, you are doing Reiki on an entire list of people, with the intent that each are receiving a complete Reiki treatment. This is a useful technique when you have a bunch of people that want distant reiki, but you do not have time to do distant healing for each. Create a list of those that want distant healing from you. On this list you can include such things as their names, ages, locations and what needs to be treated. Make sure you have permission. Once you have the list, you empower the paper with the intent that it be filled with a Reiki treatment for each. Then you simply Reiki the list. Place your hands on the paper and either just send Reiki or visualise the people receiving the treatment. Generally, doing the distant healing about 15-20 minutes is a good amount of time.

8. Declaring Yourself to be the Person

Declare to yourself that you are the person. Imagine you are the person, repeat his name thrice. Draw all the three symbols on yourself and do a full body treatment on yourself. Pray in affirmation and envision the person healed and healthy. Cover your whole body with golden light with the intention of covering him. Draw the power symbol on yourself with the intention to seal all the energies in the person.

9. On the Telephone

To do this, you use telephone/mobile phone as a bridge to your client.

Tell him that you are on phone with him and the treatment will last about for ten minutes. Ask him to close his/her eyes and feel the vibrations sitting in a relaxed position in a receptive mood.

Draw distant healing symbol once and mentally repeat the *mantra* three times. Repeat the name of your client three times. Now draw the mental healing symbol once and repeat the *mantra* three times. Draw the power symbol once and say the mantra three times.

Follow the whole body treatment. After this treatment, thank your client and wash your hands.

Other Reiki Symbols

1. ANTAHKARAN	2. OM	3. LEN-SO-MY
4. PALM MASTER	5. VASUDHA	6. OZRA
7. TU	8. INFECTION NEGATIVITY (LON SAY)	9. GA
10. PEACE	11. YOD	12. KARYA VRIDHI

13. FIRE DRAGON	14. HANG-SA	15. SATI
16. FAMILY UNITY	17. SISHUPALA	18. TRINITY
19. MIDAS STAR	20. SWASTIKA	21. NAURATRA
22. GRATITUDE	23. DESIRE	24. JAL CHAKRA

25. BALHARA	26. CHRIST LIGHT	27. INTEGRATE
28. BONA	29. AGNIPA (FIRE)	30. DRISHTI STAMBHAN
31. SANTOSH (SATISFACTION)	32. AROGYA	33. SADAGAM
34. YAHZAR	35. VAYU	36. VEL

37. TRISHUL (TRISNARI)	38. BUDDHIKARI	39. KARYA SIDDHI
40. SHAMIN	41. UDREKA	42. SHEERA
43. COURAGE	44. BILBA	45. MARA
46. JUPITER	47. DIKSHA (INITIATION SYMBOL)	48. MARY
49. OMRA	50. MOTOR-ZANON	51. JOHRE

Psychic Surgery

Negative psychic energy which is composed of negative thoughts and feelings block the flow of life force and is the cause of disease. This non-physical negative energy forms into clumps with a particular shape and lodges itself in or around physical organs, chakras or in the aura. It can be removed using this technique.

This technique can be used to facilitate the healing of any issue including physical health problems, career and money problems, emotional difficulties, relationships, addictions, mental and spiritual problems etc.

Psychic surgery can be done before regular Reiki treatment. Healing attunements can be given before the psychic surgery.

Procedure or Preparation

1. Ask the client to describe the issue he/she would like to heal.
2. Ask him to meditate on the issue to find out in which body part it is located as one generally feels tension or pain in some body part while thinking for the problem.
3. Ask him to look into the chosen area for the shape, colour, texture etc. of the problem. Remember any answer is ok.
4. Tell the client that you are going to send the problem to the God or Higher Power. Ask him to focus on the shape and meditate on letting go of it. Ask him to acknowledge and be willing to learn any lesson or receive any information related to the healing process.

The Process

1. The client can be standing or sitting in a chair.
2. Move behind the client, draw the Usui Master Symbol on both hands and clap them together three times & repeating its secret name thrice. Do the same with power symbol then draw it down the front of your body for protection, draw it over your heart and crown chakra to open them to the light.
3. Extend your Reiki fingers by pulling on your physical fingers by six to eight inches in the air. As you are pulling fingers out, breathe in through your partly closed lips, so you can hear the air flowing. Do this three times, then pat the ends of your extended fingers and imagine you can actually feel them. Draw the power symbol on the end of your extended fingers. Do this with both the hands. Move your hands around imagining you can feel the extended fingers and the power they contain.

4. Say a prayer either aloud or to yourself. Ask your Reiki Guides, the angles & archangels, all healing being of light and God to work with you to create the most powerful healing possible. Ask that the healing takes place within Divine Love & Wisdom so that the highest good is created for all concerned.
5. Draw the Power Symbol over the area of the block.
6. Stand in a powerful position and using your total strength, imagine you are reaching in and grabbing the negative energy with your extended fingers, pulling it out and sensing it up to the God. This is done with physical, emotional, mental and spiritual intention - The full strength of your being.
7. You may actually be able to see the negative shape, or use your perception to guide you in how you pull it out.
8. While pulling the negative energy out, breathe in vigorously through partly closed lips making an audible sound. Breathe vigorously while releasing the energy up to God. Imagine you are breathing into your hands and not into your lungs. Don't take the breath in, it will prevent you from pulling the negative energy into yourself.
9. Continue doing so for several minutes, you will find a change in the area, it means you are progressing. Try pulling from different angles and sides of the area. Let the area that is healing speak and guide you.
10. After 4-5 minutes ask the client how he feels or if he feels any change in the shape. If the shape is gone, you are done with this part, if it is still there partially, then continue pulling the negative energy out till its completely gone or it has been replaced with positive energy.
11. If after several sets of pulling, the negative energy is still there, you will need to communicate with the area to find out the lesson or what it needs to heal. Draw emotional/mental symbol on the area, hold your hands on the area asking from it about the guidance. Ask the client to focus on the area and say whatever comes to his mind even if it is silly, illogical or embarrassing you should also say whatever comes to mind.
12. Sometimes, you are guided to forgive someone or allowing love in. Act upon it and again pull out the negative energy and ask the client for results.
13. Sometimes, all negativities are released in the session and sometimes the process of release is started which continues on its own for several hours or days.
14. The area should be treated with Reiki & seal the treatment with.

15. Use a karate chop in the air between you both to break the connection. Retract your Reiki fingers by pushing them back as you blow out of your mouth.
16. Continue with a standard Reiki treatment using all hand positions.

The Reiki Grid

A crystal grid can be created and charged with Reiki which will continue to send Reiki to heal, protect or manifest a goal for 48 hours or longer after it is charged. In addition, the Reiki grid can be used by your guides and higher self as a bridge to transmit healing and help you and your clients.

To create your Reiki grid you will need crystals. Choose them with care and sensitivity for their intended purpose allowing your intuition to guide you to them. Your crystals should be cleansed before using them by placing in rock or sea salt or salt water for 24 hours. Say a prayer over them after they are in the salt asking that they be purified for your higher spiritual purpose. You may also attune them to the creative energies of earth, sun and moon by placing them part away in the earth with the tip pointing up during the three days of full moon. Do this in a place where the light of the sun and moon will shine on them. Say a prayer at this time asking that the creative forces of the earth, sun and moon will assist you in your highest spiritual purpose.

Next you must prepare a place for your Reiki grid. It should be a place that only you have a access to or at least a place that is your space. It could be an altar or a sacred place in your home on a desk top or self.

From the eight crystals, select the one that seems the strongest and is the most Yang or contains the most male energy. This will be your master charging crystal. Then place six of the crystals at equal points around a circle about 12" in diameter pointing inward. This will create a hexagon or six sided figure. Place the last crystal in the centre pointing to one of the others. For your central crystal, you may also choose to use a double terminated crystal, a pyramid or crystal ball. Play with the arrangement until it feels right.

Take a picture of yourself and sign your name on the back. Also draw the four Reiki symbols on the back along with their names. Include an empowering affirmation such as : I am perfectly protected and healed now on every level of my being so that my greatest spiritual purpose completely fulfilled or I allow the love and wisdom of my highest spiritual guides to protect heal and empower me to fulfill my true spiritual purpose or "Higher self guide me and heal me so that I might be of greater sense to others" or "I allow myself to heal so that my Reiki healing energies become stronger and stronger" Use any of these or any combination or use your own creative intuition to make-up your own.

After your crystals have been purified and you know how you will arrange them and your picture is prepared your next step is to charge your crystals with Reiki. Take each crystal individually and channel Reiki into it for at least ten minutes. As you do this say a prayer asking that your highest spiritual guides attune to the crystal so as to assist you in your work and in the high spiritual purpose of the Reiki grid. Also ask your highest Reiki guides as well as the angels and archangels to work with you in charging the grid. You can also do a Reiki attunement on each crystal if you have taken Reiki III to give them an even greater charge of higher frequency energy.

As you charge each crystal place it in its proper position in the grid. After the crystals are in position do not move them as this will weaken their energy connection. Then charge your master crystal in the same way.

The master crystal is to be used to keep your Reiki grid charged. Charge it with Reiki in the same way as the others. Then while holding it in your right hand begin drawing out pie shaped sections above the grid imagining energy coming from the master crystal and charging the grid. Start with the central crystal and move out to an outer crystal then across moving counter clockwise to the next outer crystal and back to the centre then back out to the same outer crystal you went in from and so on making pie shaped movements and moving around the grid in a counter clockwise direction. As you do this repeat an affirmation/mantra of power such as : "I empower this grid with light. with light. with light. to heal. to heal. to heal. I empower this grid with love. with love. with love. and wisdom. wisdom. wisdom. to heal. to heal. to heal. I call on my highest spiritual guides now to attune to this grid of light. light. light to heal. to heal. to heal. with love. with love. with love. Again I feel free to use your creative intuition to create empowering affirmation/mantras that feel right for you.

Meditate with your master crystal each day and use it to charge your Reiki grid each day. If you miss a day or two do not worry. However for your Reiki grid to remain activated you must work with it regularly. For greater strength and effectiveness do the Reiki meditation while holding your master crystal and end the meditation by projecting the four Reiki symbols into your master crystal then, use it to charge your Reiki grid.

If you have a person you would like to send Reiki to or a project or goal you would like to empower with Reiki write it out on a piece of paper and draw out the four symbols. Then Reiki it between your hands and place it within your grid. Your grid will continuously send Reiki to heal the person or manifest the goal.

Reiki Techniques

As far as Reiki techniques are concerned, we can classify them into three categories.

1. *Japanese Reiki Techniques*
2. *Western Reiki Techniques*
3. *Other Techniques*

These *meditations, exercises and techniques* will add insight, depth and power to your Reiki practice.

Japanese Reiki Techniques

Note : You can get the details of these techniques in The Reiki *Sourcebook* by *Bronwen & Frans Stiene*

- Gyoshi-Ho Technique:
- A Japanese technique for losing weight known as the Crane Method
- The Dry Bathing Technique
- The Hara Centre Technique
- Enkaku Chiryo Ho: Distant Healing
- Gyoshi Ho: A method of healing by staring
- Hado Ko Kyu Ho: A method of vibrational breathing
- Hado Meiso Ho: A method of vibrational meditation
- Hatsurei Ho: A method of generating spiritual energy
- Heso Chiryo Ho: A method of healing at the navel
- Jiko Joka Ho: A method of self purification
- Kenyoku Ho: A method of dry bathing or brushing off.
- Koki Ho: A method of sensing Ki with the breath
- Nentatsu Ho or Sei Hei Ki Chiryo Ho: A method of sending thoughts.
- Reiji Ho: A method of being guided by spirit
- Oshite Chiryo Ho: A method of using pressure with hands.
- Nadete Chiryo Ho: A method of stroking with hands
- Reiki Mawashi: A current of spiritual energy.
- Reiki undo: Movement of spiritual energy
- Seki Zui Joka Ibuki Ho: A method cleaning the spinal cord with breath

- Saibo Kassei Kokyo Ho: A method of vitalizing the cells through breath
- Tanden Chiryo Ho: A detoxifying and purifying method
- Seishin Toitsu: Creating a unified mind, soul and intention
- Uchite Chiryo Ho: A method of patting with hands
- Shuchu Reiki: (also called Shudan Reiki) In this technique several practitioners work on one person
- Ketsue Ki KoKan Ho: Blood exchange method and Zen Shin Ko Ket Su Ho is know as whole body exchange or cleansing. If the client has diabetes, reverse the direction of the sweeps beginning at the base of the spine and working up towards the neck.
- Joshen Ko Kyu Ho: Focusing the mind on one thing with breath.
- Western Reiki Techniques
- Chakra balancing
- Chakra Kassei Ko Kyu Ho: Breathing method to activate the chakras.
- Chanting: Enhancing the qualities of symbols with sound of mantras.
- Crystal Healing with Reiki
- Crystal Grid
- Psychic Surgery
- Distant Healing or distant Reiki
- Group Distant Healing
- Group Reiki: Healing with Reiki in a group
- Grounding Healing the Past and Future
- Reiki box
- Reiki Shower: A cleansing technique that increases energy flow in the body
- Scanning: Sensing imbalances in the energy field
- Smudging: Using the vibration of smell to affect energy
- Toning: A method of using the voice as healing tool.
- Dry bathing technique:
- Violet Breath: Non-traditional breath technique used with attunement process
- Hui Yin Breath: Non-traditional breath technique used with attunement process.
- Shamballa Multi dimensional healing technique.
- Golden triangle healing system.
- Talisman: A method of manifesting using an image as the focus Water
- Ritual or Mizohari: Charging water into energized healing water
- Seventh Level Technique: Activating the gateway charka that is situated where the neck meets the base of the skull.

- Power Sandwich: Increases effectiveness of hands on or distant treatments. This technique is prescribed with the belief that symbol activates other symbols.
- Reiki Aura Cleaning: Cleaning the aura of heavy energy.
- Reiki Dance
- Reiki Drumming
- Creative Visulaisation techniques
- Guide Meditation: Meet your Reiki guide and make contact with higher being Communicating with your higher self
- Antakaran: A non-traditional Reiki healing symbol.
- Reiki Boost: Balances and harmonizes the chakras allowing a greater flow of Reiki energy in the body. It is also called quick treatment.
- Spiritual response therapy (SRT): It is an ancient form of healing which operates at the soul level. Many ailments we suffer with have their energies rooted in past life and these ailments are part of our cellular memory and they re-manifest in our present life time too. By SRT we can release these blocks of cellular memory of past life negative energy.
- Reiki Essences : The Reiki essences appear to work on a very deep level. Qualified training in making, selecting and applying the Reiki essences is necessary for a Reiki Practitioner. He should also understand the healing and growth process triggered by the Reiki essences.

Other Techniques

- Candle Ritual with Rainbow Reiki.
- Crystal Fountain with Rainbow Reiki.
- Distant Healing Treatment on Telephone.
- Homoeopathic Touch with Reiki (Sai Sanjeevini).
- Lost object finding technique.
- Plant communication with Reiki.
- Reiki for Higher Self and Inner Child.
- Reiki Alarm Clock.
- Charging Bath Water, Foods & Drinks with Reiki.
- Karma Cleansing with Reiki.
- Future Situations Treatment with Reiki.
- Animal Treatments with Reiki.
- Sex with Reiki.
- Deprogramming with Reiki.
- Reiki for Electrical and Electronic Appliances.
- Activating Healing Stones.
- Glass Technique
- Cheque Technique

➤ Find Your Soulmate with Reiki

The Golden Triangle Healing System

The golden triangle healing system was developed and founded by spiritual healer and Reiki Master James Purner. This is an Egyptian energy system, you can use it to heal yourself or others. If you ask the energy to flow and close your eyes and focus on your third eye, you will either see or feel the golden triangle pyramid energy in your third eye. Now send this powerful energy towards the intended destination.

Communicating, Healing and Living with Angels in Reiki

We all have angels surrounding us constantly and our higher self is united with these angels and with God. Our higher self is in constant contact with God and the angels through the one universal mind. Your angels will guide you in every matter including healing. Feel pleasure to contact with these heavenly beings as a Reiki Practitioner. Everyone has a guardian angel with no exception. Guardian angels should not be confused with spirit guides. A Spirit Guide is a living being who has lived upon the earth in human form. Spirit guides also act in the capacity of guardian angel but the main difference is that true guardian angels never walked as mortals upon the earth and they have a higher vibratory energy frequency. Angels are beings of light who respond to our calls for guidance assistance, protection, healing and comforts.

Archangles: These are angels who supervise the guardian angels and angels upon the earth. An angle and archangels come to your assistance the moment you call them. Your request for angelic assistance should be very very sincere so that angels may appear in response to your call. There are four major archangels – 1. The Archangel Michael 2. The Archangel Gabrial 3. The Archangel Uriel 4. The Archangel Raphael whose name means God heals. Raphael is incharge of all form of healings.

You can know that angels are near. You can feel their presence when you sense warm brush across your face, shoulders, hands or arms. You can also feel their hug and the air pressure that changes when they enter in a room. You can also hear the angel's presence in a loving whisper. Quieting the mind is essential to hear angel's messages. Clairaudience is one of four ways we receive angelic assistance. Your angels may speak to you in pictures and visual images because of this clairvoyance. Each of our five senses has a corresponding spiritual senses.

Some ways to communicate with angels are : 1. Automatic writing 2. Dream 3. Divination tools 4. Oracle Cards 5. Pendulums. Ask your angels to tell you their names. You should also purify your thoughts, motives, actions, home, relationship and body. While dealing with angels people abuse alcohol and other drugs. Avoid ego ridden mind set people. Shield yourself with light and focus on love, light and truth. Supreme protector and guardian angel of the earth is Archangel Michael. You might feel Michael opening the top of your head the crown chakra area. You can also practice angel therapy in Reiki.

Akashic Records

Akashic Records is the story about your soul as it travelled through its experiences both joyful and painful in all the states in between. Information from your past can help you in your present life time also. You can find answers to your current problems and commitments or discover tools to help you create the desired changes in your life.

The term Akasha comes from Sanskrit language which means hidden library. This secret hall of records (known as Akashic Records) can be revealed by diving into the sub conscious mind in deep state of meditation.

An Akashic Record is much more than a Psychic Reading, it is a glimpse into your soul path and destiny. We each have access to this information because we are each intimately connected to the Universe. Yet sometimes the mind becomes busy and blocks the connection to this infinite internal database.

The Akasha is real. It is a sub atomic energy field of quantum particles and waves of information which are found within everything and everyone in this Universe. It is the informational highway that connects all people and all things.

The Akashic field of energy is found within each situation you are in. Just stop and look within this experience. Go through and beneath your emotions and thoughts. Notice this consciousness that is here. We are all tightly woven into the Universal web of consciousness. This is the doorway into the Akasha. When we tap into and open this sub conscious connection, we can pull up specific information about any soul's journey many places or time in history.

Telepathy

Telepathy is real. Telepathy directs mind to mind interaction independent of known senses (vision, learning, smell, taste, touch, balance and so on). Thoughts have wings but how far they can fly? Telepathy is often considered independent of distance, that is thoughts can fly as far as they desire. But is this really the case? To conclude that all telepathy is independent of distance is premature. It is extremely difficult to measure the strength of a telepathic signals apart from delivery of message. Perhaps telepathy is a non-local quantum mechanical phenomenon. Possibly there are multiple forms of telepathy, information carried on extremely low frequency, electromagnetic waves, information transferred by quantum mechanical means and information propagated via some other mechanism.

We must also consider psychological aspects of telepathy on the thoughts and emotions of someone who is psychologically near even if far removed in physical space.

Telepathic type phenomenon are not limited to the present but transcend the boundaries of time. Telepathic information can be received from the future and the past.

Emotional Vampires

Emotional vampires are dangerous to your emotional and physical health. There are many types of emotional vampires.

The first type is needy and helpless type. The needy persons often play helpless role in an effort at getting to take actions.

Depressed vampires are another type. They move slowly. Due to their extreme depressed mood they suck energy out of you and everything in the room. You can feel these types when you enter a room.

The worst is necrophilia type. This type is the depressed vampire on steroids. These types don't enjoy life at all. They carry feeling of revenge. Children raised in certain homes are often more vulnerable to these emotional vampires types.

Dealing with emotional vampires through Reiki is a wonderful technique.

Cell-Level Healing

The Bridge from the Soul to the Cell

There is a bridge between ordinary reality and spiritual reality that provides access to meditation, healing energy and wisdom. This bridge reaches directly into the units of life in the physical body, the cells. The energy of healing can touch and positively affect the inner working of the cells where the information, action, power and communication of the body does the work of life.

Bridges to healing stretch from our soul to emotions and through our minds to the teaming mass of our cells, bringing peace and vitality, joy and health.

Reach deeper and deeper into the cells of the body in order to heal and assist those who seek your help. The results are wonderful.

Healing must touch the cells because illness begins at the cellular level. The cell is basic unit of life, so healing is surprisingly powerful and effective at cellular level.

Scientific Facts about Affirmations and How to Make Them Work for You in Reiki

We should consider following 5 scientific facts on the basis of which affirmations play magic in our life.

1. Taking control of your thoughts consciously. Deep thinkers think around 50000 thoughts a day. The study show that majority of what people think is negative.
2. Affirmations are the most direct way to tap into the laws of the universe. Laws of the universe like The Law of Attraction. It is the most powerful force in the Universe and simply means that you attract what you think about – whether you want it or not.
3. You can not make anything happen in the physical universe without having the consideration first. Affirmations are vital in that they are thought that comes before action.
4. Affirmations give you confidence that you can tap into your power.
5. Scientific basis in Quantum Physics–what you think is what you manifest. Affirmations tap into that subatomic frequency because it's putting quantum energy into your thoughts. It is bringing those vibrational frequencies together - your thoughts and manifestation of them in the physical universe. Affirmations help you tap into the most basic source of creative power in the universe.

Map of Consciousness

Level	Log	Emotion	Life View
Enlightenment	700 – 1000	Ineffable	Is
Peace	600	Bliss	Perfect

Joy	540	Serenity	Complete
Love	500	Reverence	Benign
Reason	400	Understanding	Meaningful
Acceptance	350	Forgiveness	Harmonious
Willingness	310	Optimism	Hopeful
Neutrality	250	Trust	Satisfactory
Courage	200	Affirmation	Feasible
Pride	175	Scorn	Demanding
Anger	150	Hate	Antagonistic
Desire	125	Craving	Disappointing
Fear	100	Anxiety	Frightening
Grief	75	Regret	Tragic
Apathy	50	Despair	Hopeless
Guilt	30	Blame	Evil
Shame	20	Humiliation	Miserable

Vision Board

A vision board is a powerful tool that anyone can use to shape an ideal future through the power of intention and visualization.

Shock Therapy

In shock the mind stops. Conscious mind becomes inactive and subconscious mind more active. The mind becomes free of thoughts and a vacuum is created. Mind becomes receptive and any new idea or new healing can be transplanted easily.

So, use of shock therapy can also be taken in Reiki.

Love Therapy

Love is positive high frequency emotion which can heal or help us overcome many obstacles and appear to the heal. Rough reference to the emotional body, most specifically to heart chakra. The best love for healing is balanced love with compassion, acceptance and understanding. A distinction must be made between falling in love and being in love. People who are disconnected from others are roughly three times more likely to die compared to those with strong social connections. Love is more than just a feeling. It is a whole body experience. Loving and being loved improves our level of health. The greatest healing therapy is friendship and love. Nothing heals better emotionally, bio-chemically, physically and mentally than love.

Ten Ways to Raise your Vibrations

1. Gratitude: Gratitude opens your heart and connects and aligns your energy to that which you love and is good in your life.
2. Suspend judgements: Judging yourself and another lowers your energy and separates you from love, trust and joy.
3. Meditate
4. Trust
5. Honour your emotions
6. Know you are in love
7. Forgive yourself and others: It is the ultimate body-mind-soul detox.
8. Have fun
9. Love yourself and others
10. Breathing – Your breathing is an excellent way to get the energy moving in a higher vibrational way. Swing your arms and swinging your legs in a crosswise pattern. It is called a *cross crawl.* That is always moves your energy up the scale. Get more oxygen in, exhale deeply, circulate more blood to the brain. Vibe up. Now your have raised the energy and activated the attractive factor.

Hand – The Mirror of Mind

Left hand represents the subconscious and right hand represents conscious or active mind. Each hand is different because every person has a different thought patterns. Thought create bio energy so you can change your hand lines by changing your thought patterns. Human hand is also the living proof of the existence of past life.

The subconscious mind processes about 400 billion bits of information per second and the impulses travel at a speed of upto 1,00,000 mph. Compared to this your conscious mind possesses only about 2000 bits of information per second and its impulses travel only at 100-150 mph. The conscious mind is almost dim-witted cousin of the sub-conscious mind. The conscious mind can not even truly reside in the present moment. It operates only in the past or the future and has no understanding or even an inkling of the present at all. Most people simply do not get what they want to achieve because they don't believe that it will happen. Their subconscious mind instantly rejects these ideas because it has been programmed from early childhood with contradictory beliefs. So as long as your subconscious mind holds a particular belief that is not aligned with the desire you have nothing will happen.

In a nutshell, you set your goals with your conscious mind and you reach them with your subconscious mind.

The Role of Therapeutic Touch in Primal-oriented Therapy: One of the most powerful tool in psychotherapy is that of touch. The reason for it is that touch can bypass the most complicated third line defenses and takes us directly into second or even first line. (Very early memories). This is because part of the brain that registers physical touch is much more primitive than the part of the brain that registers. Emotions are rational thoughts.

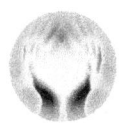

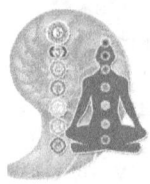

LESSON 12

Techniques & Tips

Reiki techniques are a *double-edged sword*. They are needed in order to work effectively but the moment they begin to hinder us we must let them go. When you have crossed the river, you leave the boat on the bank and continue on your way.

Four Types of Clutters

1. Physical Clutter

This constitutes piles of toys that never get played with, clothing that never gets worn, books that never get read, CDs that are never listened to, appliances that are rarely are never used and so on.

2. Paper Clutter

This is made up of piles of papers to be filed or recycled, unread piles of mails, magazines, schedules for events and activities that are no longer valid, and the like.

3. Virtual Clutter

Just because it is not taking up physical space that does not mean that it is not a clutter. Virtual clutter is in mail inboxes, unconnected computer documents, email messages, unwanted cellphone appointments and so on.

4. Mental Clutter

Any time you are feeling stressed, you are worrying, you are complaining, you are angry at someone and it is consuming your time etc then you are experiencing mental clutter. These clutters are very harmful. They suck your energy and reiki is very powerful tool to heal them.

What is Your Personal Soul Symbol

You came into physical with a personal soul symbol that lasts for your entire life time. Your soul symbol is surrounded by energy colours. All shades of all colours exist for each soul but only those necessary in the present life time will be shown. The colours in your soul symbol stay the same during your incarnation – the brightness/intensity of the colours may change or the amount of the colour may change but all the colours will stay in your soul symbol until you go back into spirit. The colours pertain to this life time only.

The Quick Coherence Technique

Step 1: Heart Focus

Focus your attention on the area around your heart, the area in the center of the chest. If your prefer the first couple of time you try it, place your hands over the center of the chest to help keep your attention in the heart area.

Step 2: Heart Breathing

Breathe deeply but normally and feel as if your breath is coming in and out through your heart area. As you inhale feel as if your breath is flowing in through the heart and as you exhale, feel it leaving through this area. Breathe slowly and casually, a little deeper than normal. Continue breathing with ease until you find a natural inner rhythm that feels good to you.

Step 3: Heart Feeling

As you maintain your heart focus and heart breathing, activate a positive feeling. Recall a positive feeling, a time when you felt good inside and try to re-experience the feeling. One of the easiest way to generate a positive heart based feeling is to remember a special place you have been to or the love you feel for a close friend or family member. This is most important step.

This quick coherence technique is very useful when you feel a draining emotion such as frustration, irritation, anxiety or stress. This technique is very useful and it takes a minute. So use it any time anywhere. It creates positive changes in your heart rhythm sending powerful signals to the brain that can improve how you are feeling. This technique helps you create a coherence state offering access to your hearts intelligence and energy.

Brainwave Entertainment

It is a technique of using external stimulation to act as a kind of timer that your brain waves fall into sync like Binaural Beats or Isochronic Tones.

These are just sounds that are specially crafted to produce a very specific pattern for the brain waves to follow that goes gently to the threshold of sleep and then quickly passes through the sleep zone. It shoots past the area where you are most likely to fall asleep.

What are Binaural Beats?
The word, *binaural means the two sounds.* You have two slightly different tones, one in each ear and when you hear them both together the difference between the two tones actually generates a third sound at a different frequency.

DNA Activation
A root for a problem is always emotional/mental and originates from your mind which is directly connected with your sub consciousness. Your sub-conscious also stores information from your past lives and your ancestral line. Through your subconsciousness, you are connected to all that is.

So, first you have to remove the roots – the solution and resolution will follow.

DNA healing will remove all the blockages and pattern actively.

Realign to your true multi-dimensional nature of love, health peace, light and happiness through DNA activation. It seeks to eliminate the physical, emotional, etheric, mental limitations, blockages and negative cycles by restoring vibration and frequency of the 12-strand DNA energy field sequence.

Crystal Acupuncture and Teragram Therapy
According to Dr Margaret there are three easy techniques to master. Hold on the acupoint and allow energy to flow from your finger tips through the crystal that amplifies your energy and sends it around your body. Next impulse if your feel nothing and wait and hold on the point until you do. Repeat these two techniques. Then when the tingling anywhere in the body rotate the crystal tip on the acupoint in a clockwise direction – like drawing a dot at the end of a sentence. This spins off the negative energy you have stored.

Reiki and Gem Stones
Following are the suitable stones along with there particular effects on the respective chakra.

Sahasrara or Crwon Chakra in Amethyst

Ajna or Third Eye chakra in Lapis Lazuli
Vishuddha or Throat Chakra in Blue Calcite
Anahata or Heart Chakra in Aventurine
Manipura or Solar Plexus Chakra in Golden Calcite
Svadhisthana or Sacral Chakra in Red Jasper
Muladhara or Root Chakra in Rainbow Obsidian

Cosmic Ordering Sequences

It is really possible to place an order with the universe. Cosmic ordering works. You have just to speak its language. It is based on the magic of asking. If you don't ask, you don't get. Asking is the first step in the manifestation process. Ask clearly and precisely. Stay focused on your desire and refuse to give it up.

Defining Psychic Powers

1. *Extra Sensory Perception*: A term coined by *Dr. J. B. Rhine*. Clairvoyance and Telepathy are two main divisions.
2. *Clairvoyance*: It is ability of seeing an event taking place far away from the subject through his or her mind.
3. *Clairaudience*: It is property of hearing sounds or voices through inner ears. In yogic practices it is known as siddhi and it manifests when throat chakra opens up.
4. *Pre-recognition*: It is free knowledge of future.
5. *Telepathy*: Ability to communicate with another person without the use of physical senses.
6. *Telekinesis*: It is movement of objects from one place to another without use of any physical force. The power of mental concentration can move objects.
7. *Levitation*: Rising into air demonstrating the weightlessness.
8. *Out of Body Experience (OBE)*: They can take place in a state of fear, stress, trauma, illness, hypnosis. Everyone have some kind of OBE during sleep.
9. *Aura*: An aura has several layers.
10. *Mediumship*: It is very practical psychic phenomena in which medium comes in contact with alleged non physical entities, be it the spirit, demi god, a spirit guide, a dead relative or God himself.
11. *Healing (Psychic or Spiritual)*
12. *Prophecy*: It is prediction.

13. *Ecstacy*: This is the ultimate level of psychic development which explodes like a volcanic eruption. It is a state of trance.
14. *Awakening*: This means new awareness. Higher universal centre called the Higher Self.

Inner Child Meditation

The inner child meditation is very powerful. It is the secret of releasing the negative emotions and blocks that keeps us away from our own abundance. Dr. Joe Vitale and Mathew Jackson has suggested this meditation by blending Ho'oponopono, hypnosis and the law of attraction. According to this technique, having a relationship with your child will heal all relationship within you. It will take you to your true source which is contentment, peace and love.

Reiki Dance

Dance is essence of human soul. All beings dance from the protozoan to human. Prayer are also carried through dance. Reiki dance is actually a dance of energy which flows through our body in rhythmic pulsing waves, bringing energizing vibrations and removing unhealthy energy. It allows us to harmonize imbalance and move freely. Dancing by itself is an active form of meditation. Reiki dance consists of various steps which can be learned.

Tips

1. *Remember, a problem well defined is a problem half-solved.* Often by clearly defining what problems appear to be, the solution immediately becomes obvious. To look deep into a problem is to be healed.
2. *If you don't like someone something, change it. If you cannot change it, change the way you think about it.*
3. *Remember, it is not what you know ... It is what you do with what you know that matters.*
4. *Grace is the beauty of the inner.* It flitters out too, but it originates from the very centre of your being.
5. He who hesitates is lost.
6. When ego asserts, Lord vanishes. When ego vanishes, Lord enters.
7. In Reiki, it is not the hand position that heals, but the position of your heart.

8. You don't have to destroy every cloud to see the sky. All you have to do is to keep remembering that you are the sky.
9. What you resist persists. Repressed emotions distort our energies.
10. *You have the world's most perfect healing machine.* You just have to know how to run it.
11. Change the texture of your thoughts and your life will change. *The future is not something we await. It is something we create.*
12. Healers do not heal, Love heals. Healers are essentially lovers – those with courage to live with an open heart and mind – allowing love to work through them. ~ Linda White Dove
13. Albert Einstein said, "The significant problem we face today cannot be solved at the same level of thinking we were at when we created them."

"You suppose you are the trouble

But you are the cure

You suppose that you are the lock on the door

But you are the key that opens it

It is too bad that you want to be someone else

You don't see your own face, your own beauty

Yet no face is more beautiful than yours."

~ Sufi Mystic Rumi

All diseases are curable, but not all patients.

www.ingramcontent.com/pod-product-compliance
Lightning Source LLC
Chambersburg PA
CBHW070337230426
43663CB00011B/2351